The PhD Application Handbook

Peter J. Bentley

Open University Press

Open University Press
McGraw-Hill Education
McGraw-Hill House
Shoppenhangers Road
Maidenhead
Berkshire
England
SL6 2QL

email: enquiries@openup.co.uk
world wide web: www.openup.co.uk

and Two Penn Plaza, New York, NY 10121–2289, USA

First published 2006

Reprinted 2010

A catalogue record of this book is available from the British Library

ISBN 10: 0335 21952 7 (pb) 0335 21953 5 (hb)
ISBN 13: 978 0 335 21952 0 (pb) 978 0 335 21953 7 (hb)

Library of Congress Cataloging-in-Publication Data

CIP data applied for

Typeset by Kerrypress Ltd
Printed in Great Britain by CPI Antony Rowe, Chippenham, Wiltshire

Contents

Acknowledgements	vii
1 Before you start	1
1.1 Why do you want to do a PhD?	2
1.2 Can you do a PhD?	5
1.3 What are your interests?	8
1.4 Do you want to be a student for another three years?	9
2 What is a PhD?	11
2.1 Different types of doctorate	11
2.2 What are the requirements of a PhD?	15
2.3 Different ways of studying	23
2.4 What do you do?	24
3 Funding	27
3.1 What fees will you have to pay?	27
3.2 Politics and money	28
3.3 UK research councils	30
3.4 UK government funding	36
3.5 Overseas Research Students Awards Scheme and the Commonwealth Scholarship Commission	37
3.6 Non-UK government funding	39
3.7 Charities	40
3.8 Industry	43
3.9 How to apply	44
4 Finding the right university	50
4.1 Old or new?	51
4.2 Where?	55
4.3 Do they do what you're interested in?	57
4.4 Research cultures	58
4.5 Judging a university	60
5 Finding the right supervisor	66
5.1 Who are they?	66
5.2 How to contact a supervisor.	67
5.3 Do you get on well with him or her?	71
5.4 How much time will he or she have for you?	73
5.5 Is he or she experienced at supervising?	75

5.6	What stage of career is he or she at?	77
5.7	Second supervisors	80
6	**Finding the right research project**	**81**
6.1	How to be different	81
6.2	Writing a proposal	83
6.3	The application form	90
7	**Securing an offer**	**96**
7.1	The interview	96
7.2	The offer	102
7.3	Student visas	104
8	**Accommodation**	**107**
8.1	What do you need?	107
8.2	Budgets	108
8.3	University accommodation	110
8.4	Private accommodation	111
9	**Beginning your PhD**	**116**
9.1	Don't believe everything you read	116
9.2	Keep careful records, and keep the records, carefully	117
9.3	Look after your finances – make a budget and stick to it	118
9.4	Remember to get your admin, reports, vivas and courses done promptly	118
9.5	Break the work into a series of smaller projects	119
9.6	Who's the first author?	120
9.7	Give credit to others when it is due	121
9.8	Listen to your supervisor and, if unhappy, talk to him or to someone else	122
9.9	Is it going to be in your thesis?	123
9.10	Insomnia happens to everyone	124
9.11	You are not the first person to do a PhD	125
9.12	Communication can be fun	126
9.13	Enjoy yourself	128
Resource Guide: current funding opportunities		**129**
1	Advertised Studentships	132
2	Small Awards	136
3	Annual Charity Studentships	139
4	UK and EU Awards	145
5	International Awards	153
6	Student Visa Guide	166
7	Directory	175
Index		**187**

Acknowledgements

Thanks to:

My PhD students past and present (Dr Jungwon Kim, Dr Rob Shipman, Dr Sanjeev Kumar, Dr Supiya Ujjin, Dr David Basanta, Dr Tim Gordon, and soon-to-be Drs Siavash Haroun Mahdavi, Boonserm Kaewkamnerd-pong, Ramona Behravan, David Malkin, Navneet Bhalla, Udi Schless-inger) for encouraging me to write this book and helping me to understand PhDs from many different perspectives. Prof. Angela Sasse, Prof. Anne Paton, Prof. Steven Hart and Dr Buzz Baum for their advice and comments at the beginning of the project. Dr Kohei Watanabe (St Edmund's College, Cambridge, and Teikyo University, Japan) for her version of 'the PhD Game'.

Dr Alex Dent, for principal investigator cartoon (originally for The *NIH Catalyst*, 1995, reproduced with permission). Udi Schlessinger for his example ORSAS form. Saoirse Amarteifio for his PhD research proposal and his comments. Dr Jungwon Kim for suggestions on foreign students. Miki Grahame for her excellent proofreading skills.

The Office of Science and Technology, UK Research Councils, the Department for Education and Skills, Association of Medical Research Charities, Royal Academy of Engineering, Royal Society, SOAS Tibawi Trust, Sasakawa Foundation, Wellcome Trust, Carnegie Trust, Lever-hulme, Arthritis Research Campaign, Ataxia Fund, British Heart Founda-tion, Cancer Research UK, Leukaemia Research Fund, Migraine Trust, Royal Society of Edinburgh, Pathological Society for permission to mention or reproduce information from their web pages. All material from UK government sources is reproduced in accordance with the Crown Copyright.

University College London and the University of London for permis-sion to reproduce text from the Graduate School student's logbook and the graduate application form.

And finally (as usual), I would like to thank the cruel and indifferent, yet astonishingly creative process of evolution for providing the inspira-tion for all of my work. Long may it continue to do so.

1
Before you start

The PhD is the highest degree available to students in the UK. But PhDs are not widely advertised in the same way as undergraduate degrees. Applying for a PhD is still a bewildering and complicated process. A surprising number of people still have no idea what a PhD is at all.

When I first heard about PhDs, I was a teenager starting my undergraduate degree. I remember walking down the university corridors and reading the names on the doors. It was a little mysterious to see 'Dr' and 'Prof' on most of them. What did they do to get those? Until then I had always thought a doctor was someone who healed you when you were sick. But they couldn't all be trained in medicine – especially in a Computer Science department!

Before long I learned of this magical type of degree that was more difficult than a Masters degree. You took no courses and had no exams – instead you did research for three years and at the end wrote a book about it, called a thesis. Then you were awarded a PhD and could write 'Dr' in front of your name. I thought it sounded great.

It was some time later when I discovered the difference between PhDs and medical doctors. I learned that the title of 'doctor' is honorary for medical practitioners, and is not recognized in the academic sense of the word. As strange as it sounds, most medical doctors do not have a doctorate. They cannot write the letters 'PhD', or 'DPhil' or 'EngD' after their names. (This is why many medical consultants – who have even more training than your average medical doctor – often revert to the title of 'Mr' or 'Ms'.)

I learned this during my own PhD, as I briefly worked alongside medical doctors in a hospital as part of my research project. When introduced to me, one doctor said with a smile, 'Oh, you're studying to become a proper doctor!' Seeing my blank expression, he went on to explain that I would earn my doctorate through three years of research, after having completed an undergraduate degree. He had only taken a single (albeit long and very difficult) undergraduate degree. I remember standing in the hospital looking around with new eyes at all the people in white coats. They weren't proper doctors – how bizarre!

Of course, I know a little more these days. I've done my PhD, and like most post-docs, have some interesting stories to tell about my experiences. I've also supervised many PhD students and helped them achieve their own doctorates. I know they have some interesting stories to tell about their experiences too.

In this book, I aim to help you achieve your ambitions. I'm not going to tell you how to do a doctorate – there are plenty of other books to guide you through the pitfalls and problems you may encounter. This book is intended to help you understand what a doctorate is and whether it is right for you. If you're happy to go ahead, it will then lead you, step by step, through the application process, helping you to choose the right university, the right supervisor and the right project. It will also help you find funding to pay for your fees and expenses throughout the course of your doctorate.

Doing a PhD can be one of the most challenging things you do in your life. One of the reasons why it is so challenging is that you must teach yourself so many new skills. By the time you're done, a PhD will no longer seem difficult. You'll know that if you began all over again, it would take you a third of the time, and you'd probably do a better job. But that's not the point. A doctorate makes you grow as a person, and the only way to get that experience is to do it. I've been through the experience myself, and have helped many students. In this book, I shall reveal all – from widely publicized requirements to secrets that academics don't normally talk about – to ensure you achieve the best start to your doctorate as possible.

1.1   Why do you want to do a PhD?

You have to be a little strange to want to do a doctorate. You'll be giving up the chance to earn some real money in a steady job, for several years of little or no money. You'll be losing the simplicity of regular hours and a boss who tells you want to do, for the complications of setting your own agenda and planning your own work.

Why do you want to do a doctorate? No, really. Why? You need to be very clear in your mind what the reasons are. Thankfully, there are some very good reasons why a normal, sane person would choose to do a doctorate. If any of these make sense to you, then you are on the right track.

1:   Wish to achieve something significant

Those who have ambitions to make money should become entrepreneurs. But if you are ambitious in that you wish to challenge yourself, push yourself to new heights or achieve a difficult goal, then a doctorate may be for you.

2:   Wish to discover or learn something new

Those who never lose their childlike curiosity of the world make great researchers. If you feel a driving force pushing you to explore and learn new things, then you may love research, and find a doctorate is perfect for you.

3:   Want to improve yourself and your life

Doing a PhD for the sake of a pay rise is not a good reason. But if you want to improve your abilities to understand and solve problems, increase your confidence, make yourself a better communicator and gain skills that may lead to a better job, then a doctorate may be right for you.

4:   It fits you

Some people are made for a doctorate. You might have grown up doing countless little 'research projects' as hobbies. You might have a natural thirst for knowledge or an insatiable appetite for reading books about a particular topic. You might have had a life-long fascination – even obsession – about something significant. If this sounds like you, and you can tailor a doctorate to suit your particular needs, then you'll love it.

Most of us have several reasons for wanting to do a doctorate, and of course they're not all good. Here are some common *bad* reasons why some people consider a PhD (and I know there was a certain amount of 'bad reason 5' that led to my own choice.)

1:   Keeping your visa

If you are thinking of a doctorate because you want to keep your student visa and stay in the UK or at your current university a little longer – don't. You must not use a PhD as a method to stay close to your friends or family, any more than you should commit a crime and have yourself locked up in jail. It is not worth it. And jail is the cheapest and easiest option by far.

2:   Peer pressure

If you're thinking of a doctorate because all your friends are going to try, well done on having some clever friends. But you will have to do the doctorate, not them. How will you feel if they all achieve their PhDs while you struggle on, year after year, getting further and further into debt?

3:   Horrible job

If you are doing a job that you hate and just want to quit – then find another job. A PhD is not an escape hatch through which you fall into a better world, it is a long steep staircase that takes extreme perseverance to climb.

4:   Fulfilling the ambitions of others

If your partner or parents think that you should do a doctorate because they wished that they had – tell them to do one themselves. It must be your own ambition that drives you, not the ambition of anyone else. Otherwise you will resent them during the tough times of your work and blame them if it goes wrong.

5:   Rebelling

If everyone is telling you to go and get a job and you don't like being told what to do, then make sure you are rebelling towards something you want, and not simply away from irritating parents or a boring town.

6:   Misplaced genius complex

If you think you are brilliant and will solve all of the world's problems, but every one of your undergrad lecturers is telling you that your ideas are unworkable and that you are not cut out for a doctorate – it is quite likely that they are right and you are wrong.

7:    *Insecurity*

You might feel that your talents are never appreciated and you crave more respect from people around you. Perhaps you like the idea of impressing them by showing a credit card with 'Dr' on it. This is not as daft as it sounds, for doctors do genuinely receive preferential treatment, and in some countries are treated with enormous respect. You are more likely to get a better job as well. However, if insecurity is your main driving force then you may struggle, for you will be surrounded by professors and post-docs who are more experienced than you throughout the course of your PhD. You will receive respect from them when you earn it, not because of the 'Dr' which they have themselves.

8:    *You've done this kind of thing before*

If you have worked in a similar area, you may have already done research or activities very similar to those that you will do during a doctorate. Or perhaps you have done a research-based project for your MSc. This is excellent experience and will help you, but a word of warning: most people think they know what they are letting themselves in for, and they are wrong. An undergraduate or MSc project does not give a proper taste of a PhD any more than a beansprout makes a Chinese meal. Working in industry is very different from academia. Even for someone with experience, the doctorate is not as easy as you might think.

Hopefully, you will find that more of the good reasons apply to you than the bad ones. Be honest with yourself. You are thinking of embarking on something that can change your life, either for better or worse, depending on you.

1.2 Can you do a PhD?

It is one thing to have some sound reasons to do a PhD. It's another thing entirely to be able to do one. Whether you can achieve a PhD is down to two things: your brain and your qualifications.

First, think about your brain. There are certain personality traits that will help you do a PhD. These do *not* include low intelligence or giving up quickly. PhD students learn how to learn. They discover that they can understand and appreciate things they previously thought were impossible. But you do need the right kind of brain to be able to cope.

Table 1.1 lists some common personality traits that many successful PhD students have in abundance. Count the ones that apply to you. If you think that at least twelve of these words describe you quite well, then you may well be the kind of person who is capable of achieving a doctorate. If you think more than twenty-five apply to you, then you will probably achieve a doctorate quite easily. If none apply to you, stop reading this book and go back to your job – you're better off doing something else. (Of course this test is more for fun than anything else, and should not be considered foolproof.)

Table 1.1 Personality traits and abilities successful PhDs often have. If you do not have them now, you may develop many of them by the time you complete your doctorate.

Intelligent	Imaginative	Methodical	Confident
Curious	Argumentative	Thorough	Controversial
Thirst for knowledge	Good concentration	Good at teaching yourself	Independent thinker
Stubborn	Dedicated	Pro-active	Ambitious
Prefer to control your own destiny	Good communicator	Bored by easy work	Desire to make a difference
Original	Literate	Dynamic	Cynical
Good at planning	Want to be the best	Self-motivating	Visionary
Can accept criticism	Willing to learn from others	Can admit mistakes	Well-organized

Assuming your brain is up to the job, the second factor is eligibility. In the UK, you are required to have the necessary experience and qualifications for the doctorate scheme you apply for. As a minimum, most UK universities require the equivalent to an upper second-class undergraduate degree (written as: 2(i)) or a score of 3.4 or better using the US system). Competition is often so fierce, however, that funded places are rarely awarded to candidates without a first-class undergraduate degree, and often a Masters degree as well. If you have a lower grade for your first degree, but have achieved an MSc, then this may make you eligible, but you will need to check with university admissions.

Universities are notoriously unwilling to be flexible about the basic eligibility requirements. It does not matter if you were a child prodigy who graduated from school six years early, published books and made millions in your own business enterprise, if you do not have the appropriate academic qualifications, they will not let you register for a PhD.

Not only should you have one or more sufficiently good first degree(s), but you should have studied in an appropriate area for the PhD topic you apply. If you have a background in Chemistry and wish to do research in Biology, you will probably find that you will not be able to obtain a PhD place. Normally, students wishing to change direction must first take a 'Transfer Masters' course – there are many run between several departments that have been designed to enable people trained in one discipline to learn a new area rapidly, for example, from Chemistry to Mathematics, or from Computer Science to Biology.

You may also find that certain PhD topics require such specialist knowledge that you will not be able to begin research without first taking a Masters course in the area. This is becoming increasingly true in the UK today most undergraduate degrees do not teach enough to enable a fresh graduate to start a PhD immediately. However, some newer doctorate schemes actually incorporate a year or two of taught material (and in some you will receive an MSc or MPhil degree for studying it) as part of the doctorate scheme. The Engineering Doctorate (EngD) and New Route PhD™ are two such popular routes.

Finally, if English is not your first language, you must have achieved a certain level of proficiency in written and spoken English language. Many English proficiency examinations exist and common requirements for PhD students are one or more of:

- TOEFL at 550–600 points or above (written paper based)
- TOEFL 225–230 or above (computer based)
- IELTS 6.5–7.0 overall (the IELTS report is only valid for two years)
- UCLES Certificate of Proficiency in English – Grade B or above
- UCLES Certificate of Advanced English – Grade B or above
- ARELS – Credit
- BEC Higher – Grade B or above

Sometimes other equivalent English qualifications may also be considered, such as:

- ULEAC (Overseas 'O' Level English)
- NEAB UETESOL
- GMAT
- Cambridge CPE (proficiency)
- Cambridge CAE (advanced)
- CCSE
- AEB Test in English for Educational Purposes (TEEP)

However, the exact requirements and recognized certifications may vary according to each university, so you must check before applying.

Even if you do satisfy the academic eligibility requirements, you are still not guaranteed an offer of a PhD place. To be successful with your application, you will need to carefully choose a university, supervisor, project, and secure funding. This is not easy – but this book will take you through your choices each step of the way.

1.3   What are your interests?

One common definition of a PhD is said to be a 'significant contribution to world knowledge'. However it is defined, it usually means that you will be a world expert on the topic when you achieve your doctorate. You will know more about that specific topic than anyone else on the planet. So make sure you are pursuing a topic that *really* interests you, or you are going to become tremendously sick of it.

Once you have got your doctorate, your area of specialization will, in the eyes of your future employers, be a way of defining who you are. It does not matter if you know a huge amount about astrophysics – if your PhD was in atomic chemistry, then that is going to be the area you will be stuck in for a while. Some post-docs who become disenfranchised with their doctoral work find it so hard to move to a new field that they take a Transfer Masters course (or even a second PhD) to prove to the world they do know about something else.

Ideally you should be looking at your PhD as a way to launch an exciting career in the area that you find most interesting. If you are planning to do your doctorate in an area suggested by your supervisor, just make very sure that you find it as exciting and worthy as he or she does. At the very least, you are also going to have to study the topic in enormous detail for at least three years – and that is really hard to do if you think the subject is boring.

You know yourself best. Think about all the courses you have taken that were the most interesting, the work you enjoyed most, your hobbies and skills. It is quite possible for a musician to go into a Computer Science department and do a doctorate in music technology, or a physicist to do a doctorate on embryogenesis in a Biology department. Don't be afraid of looking quite far afield. It is much better for you to spend another year doing a Transfer Masters and starting your dream doctorate in a new department, than to settle for something that you don't really care about and spending a lifetime working in the area.

For some people (myself included), the idea of doing more exams is abhorrent and so they are very reluctant to consider doing an MSc course before a PhD. But if you are a final-year undergraduate who really has no idea what you would like to do a PhD on (whether you have too few ideas or too many), then a Masters degree can be an excellent way to focus and explore your interests a little more before you begin the grand adventure of the PhD. The extra qualification will help your chances of obtaining a good PhD place and funding, it may introduce you to a good potential PhD supervisor, and you may even be able to publish part of your MSc report as a paper or article – a really great way to begin a PhD. It will take another twelve months, but it might make the difference between spending an easy three years on your PhD or spending a stressful five years.

A surprising number of people really do not take enough time to think about what interests them. This will be *your* doctorate, your work, your time and quite possibly your money. Make sure you do what *you* want to do. The PhD is a wonderfully flexible degree and can be shaped to suit your needs. In the worst case, you can change supervisors, funders, topics, even departments to make it fit you. But it is so much easier just to spend some time at the beginning and figure out what you would like to do.

1.4 Do you want to be a student for another three years?

PhD students are the most mature of all students. You can do a PhD at any age (I know of a retired army major who began his at age 70). In the UK, our students tend to be younger than most because we have shorter, more intense degree schemes than other countries. But even in the UK, the average age of PhD students is estimated to be between 25 and 35.

You may be married or have a family. You may have a mortgage or an expensive car. You may have elderly parents whom you need to look after. You may be living in a country that is far from your friends and family. Are you sure you want to become a student for at least another three years? Are you sure that your finances will cope? Are you sure you can cope with the food, the culture and the language? Are you sure that you can cope with living like a student for that long?

Yes, there are tricks you can use to make yourself feel better. You can call yourself a 'postgrad', a 'research associate', a 'research engineer', or a 'PhD candidate'. But you will be a student, eligible for student travel cards, student discounts in shops and student nights in the pub. You will have this status for at least three years. And the current average time taken to achieve a PhD in the UK is four years. Some people take five. Or six. Or seven. That is a long time to be poor, stressed, and suffer the indignity of being a student again. Not everyone can cope ... are you sure that you can? (See Figure 1.1 for The PhD Game.)

There will be many temptations put before you as you do your doctorate: prospects of great jobs, travel, new relationships. Some will not be compatible with your doctorate. Are you sure that you have the commitment to continue your doctorate to the bitter end, come what may? The sad truth is that the doctorate today lasts longer than many marriages and can cost more as well. No sober person would get married on a whim. So do think long and hard about your PhD. Make sure your reasons for wanting to do a doctorate are sound. Make sure you are capable of doing a PhD and that you are eligible. And make sure you do what you want to do.

0. BEGINNING Throw away sanity to start		The Ph.D Game				
1. Your supervisor gives you project title. Go on 3 spaces	**2.**	**3.** You are full of enthusiasm. Have another turn.	**4.** Realise supervisor has given nothing but project title.	**5.** Go to Library. You can't understand catalogue! Miss one turn.	**6.** The important reference has gone missing in the library. Back 2 spaces.	**7.**
14.	**13.** Things don't go well. You become disillusioned. Miss one turn	**12. End of First year**	**11.** Examiners not impressed by first year report. Throw 1 to continue.	**10.** Do extra work on first year report. Extra turn.	**9.** Supervisor makes a comment you don't understand. Back 2 spaces.	**8.** Need supervisor's help. Miss one turn finding her.
15. You become depressed. Miss 2 turns.	**16.** You become more depressed. Miss 3 turns.	**17.** Change project. Go back to beginning	**18.** Change supervisor. Throw 6 to continue. Otherwise go back 6 spaces.	**19.** Do lab demonstrations to get some dosh. Go on 2 spaces	**20.**	**21.** Lab demos take up too much of your time. Back 4 spaces.
28. You begin to think you will never finish. You are probably right.	**27.** Beer monster strikes. Spend 1 turn recovering.	**26.** Work every weekend for two months. Go on 6 spaces.	**25. END OF SECOND YEAR** No results. Who cares?	**24.** Experiments are working. Go on 4 spaces.	**23.** Specimens incorrectly labelled. Go back to 20.	**22.**
29.	**30.** You spend more time complaining than working. Miss 1 turn.	**31.** You realise your mates are earning 5 times your grant. Have a good cry!	**32.** You are asked why you started a PhD. Miss a turn finding a reason	**33.** You are offered a job. You may continue, or retire from game.	**34.** Start writing up. Now you are really depressed.	**35.**
42. Your PhD is awarded. Congratulations! Now join dole queue!	**41.** You are asked to resubmit thesis. Back to 33.	**40.** You decide PhD isn't worth the bother. Withdraw now Game over.	**39.** Harddisk crashes. Back 3 spaces	**38.** It proves impossible to write up and work. Go to 33.	**37.** Your thesis will disprove external examiners' work. Go back to 28.	**36.** Your data has just been published by rival group. Go back to 28.

Figure 1.1 The PhD Game © Kohei Watanabe, reproduced with permission.

A cynical view, but not altogether inaccurate.

2
What is a PhD?

There are actually many different types of doctorate, although this book focuses on the most common, the PhD (and research-based doctorates like it). You end up with the title 'Dr' with all of the different types, but you may have different letters after your name, for example, PhD (meaning doctor of philosophy), DPhil (also meaning doctor of philosophy), EngD (meaning engineering doctor, or doctor of engineering). The scheme may differ according to the university and the doctorate type. Engineering doctorates (and New Route PhDs™) are designed to be four-year schemes, where students take courses for the first year or two, and perform research for the rest of the time, perhaps based at a collaborating company. The traditional PhD in the UK is three years of full-time research, with no taught element. But there are more and more different types of doctorate out there, including Practice-based and Professional. You can do a PhD by thesis, by taught programme or by publication and you can study full-time, part-time, or through a 'distance learning' option. Also, the university at which you study will have differences in policy and practice with their PhDs. A doctorate at Oxford differs in important ways to a doctorate at the Open University. Knowing what those differences are and choosing the doctorate that suits you will make a big difference to your future.

2.1   Different types of doctorate

Being able to obtain a doctorate in your twenties is a modern idea. Originally, the title of 'Doctor',[1] and specifically 'Doctor of Philosophy'[2]

---

[1]   'Doctor' is from the Latin, meaning teacher.
[2]   The word 'Philosophy' comes from the Greek words *philos*, meaning love, and *Sophia*, meaning wisdom.

was a rarely awarded recognition of an individual who had spent his life dedicated to learning and knowledge. Such recognition could only be given after the person had spent sufficient time in their career, so the youngest doctors were always middle-aged.

With the growth of the sciences, pure philosophy began to wane, and so the recognition of Doctor of Philosophy (PhD) was quietly forgotten by some universities. But in the nineteenth century, the PhD re-emerged with a new role (at the Friedrich Wilhelm University, in Berlin). Now, it was a degree to be awarded to an individual who had performed original research in the sciences or humanities – a lesser requirement than the original PhD. This new PhD was taken up by American universities and eventually spread to the UK in the early twentieth century.

When it reached the UK, it caused a certain amount of confusion in the nomenclature. Some UK universities, such as the University of St. Andrews, dropped their existing higher doctorate (the DPhil) and replaced it with the research-based PhD. Others, such as Oxford and Sussex, retain the name DPhil for research-based doctorates to this day.[3] To make matters more complicated, despite the arrival of the PhD, the idea of a doctorate awarded for lifetime achievement was not forgotten in the UK. So today we have the concept of normal or junior doctors such as the PhD, which are available to students, and the higher doctorates, which are awarded often after examination of more than 10 years of research effort beyond the PhD. Table 2.1 lists some of the higher doctorates available today. You cannot explicitly study for such degrees, so this book will focus on the normal doctorates.

In the UK, all doctoral students must be graduates – they must have at least one degree already (and typically two – a bachelors and a masters). In countries such as USA, it is possible to study for a first-degree or first-professional doctorate. Because they are awarded for a single degree, without research, they are considered lesser than the normal doctorate. Table 2.2 lists some of the contemporary first-degree doctorates available.

Today there are surprising numbers of different doctorate schemes. All are considered to be equally valuable (although you may find a certain snobbery and distaste from the older universities if you have one of the very new, non-research-based doctorates). Table 2.3 lists some of the current doctorate schemes available. Many require students to spend a significant amount of the time taking advanced courses. Some require demonstration of practical skills to a high level. If you are thinking of a

---

[3] There are also some other letters you may see after 'PhD'. The term 'PhD (ABD)' is not used in the UK, but is becoming common in USA, and means 'all but dissertation'. This really means that the student has not yet been awarded a degree of PhD – he or she has completed his/her coursework and examinations but has not submitted a thesis yet. In some universities, the student can write a preliminary thesis and be awarded an MPhil (Master of Philosphy) degree, before submitting the full PhD thesis. Alternatively, sometimes a university grants an honorary PhD or DA, or other doctoral degree, with the added designation of *honoris causa* ('for the sake of honour', in Latin), or 'Drhc'.

Table 2.1 Higher doctorates

Divinitatis Doctor or Doctor of Divinity (DD)	Legum Doctor or Doctor of Laws (LLD)
Doctor of Civil Law (DCL)	Scientiæ Doctor or Doctor of Science (DSc or ScD)
Literarum Doctor or Doctor of Letters (DLitt or LittD)	Musicæ Doctor or Doctor of Music (DMus or MusD)
Doctor of Literature (DLit)	Doctor of Dental Surgery (DDS)
Medicinæ Doctor or Doctor of Medicine (MD or DM)	Doctor of Technology (DTech)
Doctor of the University – honorary (DUniv)	

Table 2.2 First-degree (or first-professional) doctorates

DC (Doctor of Chiropractic)	DDS (Doctor of Dental Surgery)
J.D. (Juris Doctor or Doctor of Law)	MD (Medicinæ Doctor or Doctor of Medicine) (US)
DPT (Doctor of Physical Therapy)	DO (Doctor of Osteopathic Medicine)
DPM (Doctor of Podiatric Medicine)	DMD (Doctor of Dental Medicine)
DVM (Doctor of Veterinary Medicine)	PsyD (Doctor of Psychology)
PharmD (Doctor of Pharmacy)	OD (Optometry Doctor or Doctor of Optometry)

doctorate that involves courses, you must make sure you obtain the information from your university about which courses you need to take and which skills you need to demonstrate, so you can choose the right options for yourself.

In the UK, taught or professional degrees are considered to be those that involve a taught element for more than one third of the time. In contrast, practical degrees require the production of an original artefact in addition to, or in some cases, instead of the written thesis. Such degrees are favoured by artists, designers and musicians, but also include disciplines such as software design, engineering and law. There is still some debate about how standards should be maintained in professional and practical doctorates, with numerous UK government reports attempting to clarify the issues. For now, individual universities are setting their own standards.

A recent government report suggested that UK doctorates should have four main aims:

1   research and scholarship;
2   preparation for research and deepening subject knowledge;
3   conversion, and
4   professional and practice-related.

Table 2.3 Types of doctorate

Doctor of Arts (DA)	Doctor of Architecture (DArch)	Doctor of Applied Science (DAS)	Doctor of Business Administration (DBA)
Doctor of Chemistry (DChem)	Doctor of Criminal Justice (DCJ)	Doctor of Comparative/Civil Law (DCL)	Doctor of Computer Science (DCS)
Doctor of Criminology (DCrim)	Doctor of Education (EdD)	Doctor of Environmental Design (DED)	Doctor of Engineering (DEng)
Doctor of Environment (DEnv)	Doctor of Engineering Science (DESc/ScDE)	Doctor of Forestry (DF)	Doctor of Fine Arts (DFA)
Doctor of Geological Science (DGS)	Doctor of Hebrew Literature/Letters (DHL)	Doctor of Health and Safety (DHS)	Doctor of Hebrew Studies (DHS)
Doctor of Industrial Technology (DIT)	Doctor of Information Technology (DIT)	Doctor of Juridical Science (SJD)	Doctor of Liberal Studies (DLS)
Doctor of Library Science (DLS)	Doctor of Music (DM)	Doctor of Musical Arts (DMA, A Mus D)	Doctor of Musical Education (DME)
Doctor of Ministry (DMin/DM)	Doctor of Modern Languages (DML)	Doctor of Music Ministry (DMM)	Doctor of Medical Science (DMSc)
Doctor of Nursing Science (DNSc)	Doctor of Public Administration (DPA)	Doctor of Physical Education (DPE)	Doctor of Public Health (DPH)
Doctor of Professional Studies (DPS)	Doctor of Design (DrDES)	Doctor of Religious Education (DRE)	Doctor of Recreation (DRec/DR)
Doctor of Science (DSc/ScD)	Doctor of Science in Dentistry (DScD)	Doctor of Science and Hygiene (DScH)	Doctor of Science in Veterinary Medicine (DScVM)
Doctor of Sacred Music (DSM)	Doctor of Social Science (DSSc / SocSciD)	Doctor of Social Work (DSW)	Doctor of Canon Law (JCD)
Doctor of the Science of Law (LScD)	Doctor of Rehabilitation (RhD)	Doctor of Sacred Theology (STD)	Doctor of Theology (ThD)
Doctor of Clinical Psychology (DClinPsych)	Doctor of Educational Psychology (EdPsychD)	Doctor of Nursing Science (DNursSci)	Doctor of Health Science (HScD)
Doctor of Philosophy (PhD / DPhil)	Engineering Doctorate (EngD)		

But the different types of doctorate do not achieve these aims well. According to the Harris Report, the professional doctorate addresses aims 2 and 4. The traditional PhD and newer EngD addresses aims 1, 2 and 4. It is not clear which aims are tackled by the practical doctorate. No type of doctorate was identified that provided the 'conversion' element of aim 3 – but most universities would argue that the objective of a doctorate is to specialize and not to convert to a new area.

Luckily, research-based doctorates are very well established and well understood. For the rest of this book, we shall concentrate on the most common types of doctorate, the PhD – also known as the DPhil and sometimes, the EngD.

2.2 What are the requirements of a PhD?

There is a standard definition of PhD research that has been widely accepted by most UK universities. Written by the Council for National Academic Awards in the UK, it suggests that:

> The PhD is awarded to a candidate who, having critically investigated and evaluated an approved topic resulting in an independent and original contribution to knowledge and demonstrated an understanding of research methods appropriate to the chosen field, has presented and defended a thesis, by oral examination, to the satisfaction of the examiners.

This somewhat clumsy sentence does indeed encapsulate a PhD very well. Regardless of the field, each of those elements must be satisfied before you will achieve your PhD. You will have to choose a topic on which to focus, and this will have to be approved by the supervisor and department. You will have to show that you can critically investigate and evaluate the work of others and the work of yourself in the area. You will have to work independently and not require anyone to tell you what to do. You will have to show some form of originality, usually in the form of an original contribution to knowledge. You will have to show that you know how to do appropriate research properly on your topic. You will have to write a thesis in which you demonstrate all of these elements. You will have to defend the thesis orally in front of examiners – often known as a defence, viva voca,[4] or simply the viva. The examiners will be experts (typically independent professors) in the field, and you will have to satisfy those experts that you have achieved every one of the points above.[5]

There is also widespread agreement about the qualities that a PhD should demonstrate. These were summarized in another of those government reports. Let us look at each of the eight points listed in the report in turn and see what it means:

An original contribution to knowledge and/or understanding

You obviously have to achieve something significant during a PhD, and from an academic perspective, perhaps the most useful thing you can do is to increase the sum of human knowledge. Anything else will be transitory and lost or forgotten within a few months. Knowledge is preserved and incorporated into new methods, beliefs and practices. Really significant understandings will become part of human culture and will be preserved for centuries.

Exactly what your contribution to knowledge is will depend entirely on your chosen area. It might be a new mathematical proof, a new interpretation of a musical score, a new way of controlling robots, a new analysis of a historical document, or a new understanding of the function of a particular protein in a specific organism. Whatever it is, you will almost certainly have to write it down in some length and considerable detail in your thesis. This is how it becomes a contribution to knowledge – you record your efforts for the world in your thesis, enabling others after you to continue and improve in the same area.

Undertake a systematic enquiry

When you do your PhD, you have to learn how to do research. Whether you are working in the sciences or in the arts and humanities, you must perform research in a methodical and systematic way. For example, if you are trying to understand the impact of mobile phones on our culture during the last ten years, you cannot just chat to your friends about their

---

[4] From the Latin meaning *by live voice*.
[5] In some fields the viva may take the form of the Scandanavian *disputation* where an expert takes the role of opponent and the student takes the role of respondent, in a public debate open to all. A grading committee then decides on the final result. In countries such as the Netherlands and the USA it is typical for the viva to take place in front of a thesis committee and larger audience, but the thesis has already been approved and the defence is viewed more as a formality or tradition. In Australia, the decision is made by the committee without any viva at all.

experiences. You will need to understand what existing research has been done in the area (which will involve reading research papers and possibly other people's PhD theses). You will need to analyse exactly what your problem is – which people use mobile phones and why? Do people of different ages, nationalities or cultures use different phones and if so why? How has this pattern changed? How does the influx of new models affect people and how do people affect the design of new models? Does new technology in phones change the behaviour of people and if so how? And so on.

Learning how to undertake a systematic enquiry is one of the cornerstones of a PhD. In the sciences, it is essentially your training to become a fully-fledged scientist. By the end of your doctorate you will have the skills necessary to enable you to investigate almost anything. You will understand the importance of gathering reliable evidence to support any claim, and you will probably become rather more cynical about the world as you realize that many 'truths' are not supported by sensible evidence.

Apply methods appropriate to the subject

It is common for PhD research to be very proactive. You will not always be able to just use an Internet search engine and find some answers. You will often have to go digging for the evidence. In the sciences, this often means that you will have to either calculate an answer or perform experiments and then analyse the results. This may well involve learning a vast set of skills in mathematics and computing, experimental practice, and the use of highly specialized scientific equipment. In the arts and humanities, you will have to learn how to understand and analyse material in the appropriate way, and you may need to learn about psychology, statistics, and other cultures or languages. By the end of your PhD you will be a world expert in your area. You are thus expected to be an expert in the methods used in your area.

A grasp of context

One of the most common failings of all PhD students is a poor awareness of the context of their work. A question about the broader context of the work is actually one of the normal questions asked by the examiners during the viva. It may seem strange that someone who has worked for years on one narrow area can forget how his or her work relates to the outside world. But as students specialize and focus, it is normal for their concentration to become so intense that everything else seems like an irrelevant distraction.

It is, of course, essential that students recognize that their work will be perceived and exploited differently by different people. This is especially true in our media-driven world where, for example, a focused study of the effects of a gene on obesity might result in crazy headline stories if the results are not reported carefully.

It is also essential that students learn that their work will fit into the ever-growing jigsaw puzzle of other research being performed. They need to become aware of exactly what is being done in their area – and related areas – and ensure they build upon or exploit anything appropriate. It is devastating to have your examiners tell you that your 'original' work is a duplication of the work of someone five years ago in another country. In the worst case, it might prevent you from obtaining your doctorate. But it may happen unless you do a thorough literature survey.

Most PhD students will read several hundred articles and books during the course of their research. The number can be so high that it is very easy to lose track of what you read and what you thought of each document. My standard piece of advice for all students is: keep a record of everything you read. Write down the title, where you got it, what it is about, and what you thought of it. Keep it on your computer so that you can search it and copy and paste. And for goodness sake, back it up!

Documentation and communication in a permanent form

The thesis is obviously the most visible way in which you record and document your work. In many universities, there is a requirement for the thesis to be 'of publishable quality' and indeed, some post-docs will even publish their thesis as a book. However, most PhD students are expected to do much more than just a thesis. During the course of the work, it is usual for you to write articles or scientific papers. It is expected that you will present your work orally at conferences or exhibitions. It is normal for you to meet and get to know many of your peers at these events, and they will be very useful in obtaining feedback about your work, and providing more options for your career after your doctorate.

Publishing your work in peer-reviewed conferences or journals can be a very useful trick to vouchsafe your work and smooth your viva. Peer-review means that independent experts will read and check your work before it is accepted for publication. It is common for detailed critiques to be given, often requiring corrections to be made. If accepted in a credible publication, the work is much safer and less likely to be challenged by your examiners in the viva. Publishing all your major results often makes the viva easy, and can make writing the thesis much easier as you will have written much of the material already. Publishing frequently also helps break the work up into a series of smaller projects with clear deadlines and outcomes – this is often very helpful to keep you working at a fast pace. Unfortunately, not all fields are suited to this approach. Fast-moving fields such as engineering and computer science are great for rapid publishing. But the biological sciences often require so much time to perform experiments and generate results that publishing becomes a slow and careful process.

In some areas, such as the arts or architecture, you will be expected to generate physical artefacts which may be exhibited and undergo critique. This process can be quite disheartening when criticisms are severe and seemingly unrelenting. Nevertheless, in these fields it is the method used to teach, and so you have to learn to endure all criticism without taking anything personally.

In all areas, it is vital that a careful record is made of all work. The most important thing is for you to be able to explain how you achieved what you did, and why you made the decisions that you did. It may not be the most exciting aspect of the work, but keeping a careful and detailed record of everything is essential. You will forget the detail of what you did a couple of years ago, so you will not be able to write your thesis without your notes. And even if you have a wonderful memory, that is no use to anyone else. Only by writing everything down can you record your activities for posterity and communicate them to others.

Sustained and contextualized logical argument

A PhD thesis has the name for a reason. A thesis is an argument – a position that you take. The core is often phrased as a hypothesis – a theory which requires evidence to prove or disprove it. In the arts and humanities it is common to write a 'PhD dissertation' which may have a less formal structure. But in all fields, there is the concept that you should present an argument or point of view in your thesis. This must be very clearly explained.[6] There will usually be at least one, and sometimes several chapters of the thesis that describe context by way of critical review of related literature. The whole of the thesis should be viewed as a body of evidence, gathered by you using sound research methods, to support your argument. Your evidence should be fair and should address all possible counterarguments. It should also be logical – you need to demonstrate an ability to reason clearly and carefully.

By the end of the PhD, you should be able to tell the difference between a well-argued hypothesis and one that is weak and not to be trusted. You

---

[6] In fact, it is common for the title of the work to summarize the central argument or hypothesis, often by simple rewording. For example, a thesis with the central hypothesis 'Liquid crystal enables reconfigurable computation' might have the title 'Reconfigurable Computation Using Liquid Crystal'.

> *Argument*
> Computer games cause homelessness.
>
> *Justification*
> Computer games show excessive violence.
> Teenagers play too many computer games.
> Thus teenagers have more violent tendencies.
> Parents of violent teenagers are more stressed.
> Stressed people are more likely to turn to alcoholism.
> Alcoholics are more likely to have gambling problems.
> Gambling addicts often lose their homes.

Figure 2.1 A poor argument may be made from a string of seemingly logical steps. This example may be clearly ludicrous, but if each of these steps was some terminology-laden and 'proven' scientific finding, would you still spot it as a poor argument?

should also be able to explain exactly why an argument makes no sense – like the seemingly logical, yet flawed argument in Figure 2.1.

Justification of actions in relation to process and product

You will not be able to justify all of your actions sensibly to begin with. It takes a while to learn how to plan your time and make appropriate choices during the doctorate. All students end up doing things they do not need to. The important thing is to have a good supervisor who will tell you when you have gone off track, and for you to be able to listen and trust that advice. Insecurity is very common for PhD students. Many are not sure they have done the right thing or that they have done enough to justify their PhD.

It is also common for supervisors to be ignored and for the students to pursue blind alleys and dead ends. At some point you will probably convince yourself that a certain course of action is appropriate and will pursue it against advice given to you. It is only when you find yourself drifting several months later, feeling lost and alone, that you realize that maybe the advice was right and you should not have gone that way.

In reality, every doctorate is a confusing and sometimes depressing series of choices of what to do next. Most of us may know where we want to go, but the PhD is all about learning how best to get there. You cannot learn without making a few mistakes along the way. Don't be fooled by the wonderfully coherent nature of PhD theses that you may read. Every student had some significant problems along the way. The trick is to write the thesis in such a way that the actions you took seem sensible and appropriate – if necessary by omitting the irrelevant work altogether.

By the end, you will realize that a PhD is much easier than you first thought – mainly because you will understand exactly what you need to do. You will understand what justifiable actions in research are, and you will probably have first-hand experience of what unjustifiable actions are.

Valid and original work of high quality

This is perhaps the most obvious of requirements for a PhD. Judged by your examiners, who will know the area as well as you, you need to achieve something that is considered valid (that is without mistakes), original (that no one has done before) and of high quality (that is, of PhD standard; and more substantive than MPhil or MRes work). If you can publish some of your work before you submit the thesis, you will get an idea of what your peers think of your work. Be assured that if you make any mistakes, you are unoriginal, or the work is low quality, you will hear about it!

Your last line of defence is provided by your supervisors. They will not let you submit anything that does not meet these requirements, so do make sure you listen to them and make any corrections they recommend before submitting.

These general qualities are intended to be applicable to all PhDs in the UK. Nevertheless, there is a growing feeling that arts and humanities PhDs may have different styles and motivations. In some cases there is a misconception that science-based PhDs are 'awarded in recognition of research and discovery, not creativity'. This is patently nonsense – *all* PhDs involve notable creativity, whether the contribution is in mathematics or in art. The best scientists are wonderfully creative people, and the best artists are often so technically gifted that they are effectively scientists. However, those working in the arts and humanities have created some definitions of PhD research more relevant for these fields:

> It must define a series of research questions that will be addressed or problems that will be explored in the course of the research. It must also define its objectives in terms of answering those questions or reporting on the results of the research project.

This is actually important for PhDs in all fields. You cannot have a coherent thesis if you do not identify your focus. One of the most effective ways of planning your time is to write down your main argument, then break it down into a series of research questions that need to be addressed. Your objectives will then form clearly identified steps leading you to coherent answers to those research questions. It is very common for PhD theses to be written using this kind of framework. Often the introductory chapter will outline the argument or hypothesis, the related research questions, and will list the objectives. Then in the conclusions, each objective is revisited, with a summary of how it was satisfied and where in the thesis this was described. The evidence to support the research questions and overall argument is then summarized, leading to the final culmination – you proved your point!

In the arts and humanities, there may not be a single argument, but instead there might be a series of related research questions. This is sometimes referred to as a 'portfolio thesis' – it might cover a broader range of questions than is typical in the sciences.

> It must specify a research context for the questions to be addressed or problems to be explored. You must specify why it is important that these particular questions should be answered or problems explored; what other research is being or has been conducted in this area; and what particular contribution this particular project will make to the advancement of knowledge, understanding and insights in this area.

Again, this series of requirements is equally valid for all PhDs. As we saw with the earlier 'grasp of concept' theme, it is important to relate your work to the work of others in the area, and to the outside world as a whole. The more relevant you can make your work to people, the more significant it will become.

Being cynical, some advice I usually give to students at the start of their PhD is: choose your research topic carefully. If you pick an area that is already very popular, then you may find it difficult to stand out from the crowd. Another PhD thesis among a flock of similar ones is not really noticeable. If you pick an area that is stagnating, you will be seen as old-fashioned and out of date. That will not be good for your future career. The trick is to find an area that is just emerging – maybe there have been a few publications, but hardly any PhDs on the topic. Then you might have the opportunity to 'stand at the crest of the wave' – your thesis will be the first in the area and you will become very well known. It is a hard trick to manage and more often than not you will find several others are trying to do the same as you, so you may have some competition. You need the advice of a good supervisor who can tell you what is hot and what is not. It may seem strange, but new ideas are really like new fashions – if you can make yourself fashionable (or even be the new fashion designer) – then you may be able to launch a successful and lucrative career. It's all about knowing the area and what is going on in it.

> It must specify a methodology for addressing and answering the research questions. You must state how you are going to set about answering the questions that have been set, or exploring the matters to be explored.

In science-based PhDs there is very little freedom in choice of methodology. You must follow scientific method or your results will not be believed. This should not be seen as a constraint – science is our most effective methodology for finding out the truth. Through scientific method we learn to gather reliable evidence to support or refute our hypotheses. It is the ultimate in cynicism: you want me to believe something? Well, give me solid evidence to prove you are right. If you cannot, I won't believe you.

In the arts and humanities, things can be a little different. It is very hard to prove that the emotion felt by a long-dead painter led to the emergence of a new style. And it is hard to measure how subjective feelings produced by a personal journey through a trauma influenced the writing of a famous poem. It is therefore essential for the methodology to be explicitly identified and described, for it will be this framework that you must work within. To do this, you need to understand where your evidence comes from, for example in the study of film, is it the views of film critics and if so, which ones? How and why do you pick your material; how do you judge its quality, reliability and consistency?

At a fundamental level, all PhDs should make this point clear. All research relies on a series of assumptions and accepted truths. For example, the fact that empirical experiments may show that penicillin kills a type of bacterium successfully in every one of ten million trials does not prove that it always will, any more than my observation of the sun rising each day proves it will rise tomorrow. We must make certain assumptions about likelihoods and, for any claim made in any discipline, we should always be clear about how those assumptions may affect its validity.

2.3 Different ways of studying

The standard PhD takes an average of four years to complete in the UK. You may live at or near to your university for most of this time, and may spend a significant proportion of the time at the university in a laboratory or office provided for your use. Often, the equipment needed for the research will be provided by the university and one or both supervisors will be staff based in the same department. There will also be technicians, secretaries and many other support staff who will assist you should you need it. You will have access to libraries and will be able to participate and collaborate with research groups and experts in their university. From the perspective of the university, all of these facilities cost money. So even if you never attend a single lecture again, your PhD fees are needed to cover the cost of equipment, space and time of the staff who assist you.

But you do not have to study full time. If you are working and would prefer to do your PhD part time, then most universities will allow you to register as a part-time student. This may have significant advantages: because you may rarely use the university facilities (indeed, you may not be given an office or space in a lab), the fees are usually a fraction of the cost for full-time students. You will also have much more time to complete your doctorate – part-time PhDs are often allowed five or six years instead of three. But there is a downside. Most universities prefer not to take on too many part-time PhD students because statistically, the success rate is very low. With reduced access to the university facilities and staff, distractions from work, and so many years in which to lose motivation and direction, most part-time students give up and never achieve their PhDs.

There are several other options, some better, some worse. One interesting variation is offered by the Open University. If you are living in the UK, you can register to become an 'external part-time student', and find yourself a first supervisor at the university whom you would see every few months. Your research is then performed at a collaborating institute or university (at your own cost), which could be one of many in the UK. A typical student might be a researcher in a UK lab who could use the facilities to do his or her own research for some of the time without extra cost. Because the Open University does not host the student, the fees are tiny (£119 per quarter in 2005) and you are only charged the home student rate if you are living in the UK – a significant advantage if you are not a UK or EU citizen. But of course, as a part-time foreign student you must have a work visa to stay in the UK, and a steady job. You cannot use a part-time studentship to keep a student visa. And even with such a good deal, the Open University still finds that many part-time students either give up, or register to become full time after a while.

2.4   What do you do?

Almost no one begins their PhD knowing what to do. The first few days are always a little scary. If your doctorate has a taught element, you may find the transition easier – you will be back in the lecture theatres receiving more of those familiar lectures you had in your previous degrees. If your doctorate involves practical skills, you may find yourself in a new lab or studio, learning about the equipment and getting to know your new colleagues.

Practically, a PhD may involve a lot of reading, quite a bit of writing, and a lot of practical research in your office, lab or studio. (We saw in Section 2.2 the kinds of activities that count as PhD research.) If you are lucky, it may also involve regular stimulating interaction with your supervisor, fellow students and colleagues as you brainstorm or discuss ideas. If you do well, it should involve travel around the world to international events such as conferences or exhibitions. Most universities will provide financial support for this kind of travel, so do not be afraid to make use of it – some of my students have managed to travel the world extensively and have a great time while presenting their work at conferences. (I have been known to attend the odd conference in Australia and Hawaii myself, as well.)

Exactly what your day-to-day activities are will depend on the subject you study and the research culture of the university in question (see Chapter 3 for more details). In some fields it is common for you to be expected to follow your supervisor's instructions closely and to take on regular duties in a lab. In other fields you may be expected to work autonomously with little contact with your supervisor.

Although it may not feel like it at the time, the day-to-day activities are much less important than the generic skills you learn. The point of a PhD is to make you a professional in your area. By the end of a science-based PhD, you will have learned how to be a scientist. By the end of a history-based PhD you will have learned how to be a historian. (You get the idea.) Your job during your research is not necessarily to cure cancer (although that would be great, so don't be afraid of trying). Your job is actually to learn a series of skills that will change you, give you confidence, and enable you to do whatever you want to with your life. You will learn how to question and how to find things out, how to pose research questions, how to formalize an idea as a hypothesis, and how to prove or disprove it by gathering evidence. Not all doctorates are the same – a PhD in the arts will teach you some subtly different skills to a PhD in science. But in all doctorates you will learn how to communicate clearly, both orally and in writing. You will become a world expert in your area, and may even gain a bit of fame along the way. You will be highly proficient in the methods and equipment used in your field and you will acquire the ability to critically evaluate the work of yourself and others.

You will also learn how to learn. This may seem a strange thing to read, but it is true. At the start of your doctorate there will be a lot of articles or books that you may find confusing or nonsensical. After a couple of years, when you re-read the same material you will find it suddenly seems simple – maybe even naïve. Your brain gets used to absorbing new information and learning becomes faster.

The other part of doing a PhD is the emotional side. Most of us invest a great deal of our emotional energy in our work. If something goes right, we are elated and thrilled. If something goes wrong, it really matters to us. Those who achieve their PhDs always feel as if they are members of a club. They know that they have gone through hell and back to get their doctorate. They know that they've suffered emotionally, lost sleep, become depressed, thought about giving it up, but carried on anyway. Post-docs have a sense of camaraderie because every PhD represents the achievement of overcoming extreme stress, self-doubt and worry.

The stress comes from several sources. Some of it may be from your supervisor pushing you to do better, or peer pressure from your friends. Our families also can be very proud of their partners or children undertaking such an impressive course. The pressure you receive from your proud mother's words, 'my son is going to be a *doctor!'* can be hard to get away from. Financial pressure is another common feature of doctorates. Worrying about paying your rent does not help you concentrate on work. But in reality, the stress you will experience from your PhD is insidious because you pile it on top of your own head. You decide what you are going to do, so it's your own fault if it goes wrong or it's not good enough. You kick yourself much more than anyone else when you don't achieve what you planned to. You cannot get away from yourself, or blame a boss or an annoying client, so you cannot escape the stress. Feelings (and often physical symptoms) of stress are so common and normal in good PhD students that I worry if one of my students shows none of them – it probably means they are not working (or caring) hard enough.

Most PhD students who give up their doctorates do so because they have become depressed, disenfranchised or lack the motivation to finish, rather than because they lack the intellectual capacity. They feel as if they are unable to make progress, or that everything they have done is worthless. One of your biggest challenges during your doctorate is to avoid thinking like that. You need to remember that the PhD is about learning skills, not just producing a thesis. Even if you have spent two years doing work that you don't think will make it into the thesis, you have learnt a huge amount about research, writing, communication and critique in that time. So your ability to do good work faster will be improved. Also, remember that all knowledge is useful – learning how *not* to do something (even if that was not your intention) can be more important than providing one way of doing it. There is no reason why such knowledge cannot form an important part of your thesis.

A PhD can be a wonderful, life-changing experience. It is a way for you to prove to yourself and to the world that you can achieve something significant. Stay positive, focused and committed, and you'll achieve your ambition.

3
Funding

The most common reason why PhD candidates are unable to begin a doctorate, or are forced to finish it, is lack of funding. Universities require PhD fees to be paid each year, and may also charge late fees if you take too long to finish. You will also need money to pay your rent, travel and live on. If you come from overseas, the total cost of a doctorate can be in excess of £100,000 – a horrifying amount of money. Your aim should be to achieve sufficient funding to cover the entire cost of your doctorate. It may not be easy, but your doctorate does not have to mean financial debt.

3.1   What fees will you have to pay?

College fees are charged by universities in order to cover the cost of equipment, the use of facilities and tuition costs. They are different for every university, and sometimes for each department in the university. Often, the older universities such as Oxford, University of London, and Cambridge will charge much more than newer universities such as the University of Huddersfield or the University of East London. The older universities argue that their better facilities, greater number of staff, more experienced staff and better research output simply cost a whole lot more. Of course, the 'younger' universities complain of unfairness and point out that they dedicate more time to teaching, so their undergraduate students may be able to study rather more contemporary and modern courses.

Your choice of university should not be made on fees alone, but it is worth remembering that (unless you need specialized laboratory equipment) you will be able to do your PhD almost anywhere, and it will be considered equally good wherever you do it. Some still believe that a PhD from Imperial College London is better than one from, say, the University of Essex. This is not necessarily true – a PhD must be assessed by external examiners and so the standards of PhDs across the UK are generally very consistent. That doesn't mean that they're all good, but it does mean that you cannot point to one university or department and find all good or all bad PhDs. Some lousy doctorates are passed in our best universities and some wonderful doctorates are passed in some rather less prestigious universities. (We look at universities in more detail in Chapter 4.)

As well as varying by university, the fees also vary according to your nationality. For example, if you are a UK or EU citizen, you may have to pay around £3000 a year to study in the UK. But if you are an overseas student (that is, not from the UK or the EU), then you may have to pay £13,000 a year at the same university. Normally it is essential that you obtain funding to pay the fees. Working while doing a PhD is rarely sensible (unless the university employs you), and taking out loans is a great way to get very stressed.

The fees for a university can sometimes apply for all departments, regardless of the differences between them. This may not always seem fair. For example, the fees for PhDs in the humanities may be pretty much the same as for science-based PhDs, but because the financial turnover of the departments may be dramatically different (a biology department may have a turnover 100 times that of a history department), the students may receive dramatically different support for their money. It is common for PhDs in the humanities not to be given any office space or equipment. Because these doctorates involve considerable amounts of reading, the fees are generally intended to cover library access and supervisor staff costs. Humanities students may spend much of their time in the library or working at home. Contrast this with science-based PhDs who pay the same, but often receive office space, laboratory use, their own equipment and substantial travel support. The general rule is: a department working in areas directly useful to medicine, technology or industry is likely to be quite rich. A rich department can afford to give its PhD students rather more. This does not mean that poor departments are bad. It just means that their work attracts less money. There is a place in our world for both studies of Chaucer and cures for cancer; the latter will always receive more money compared to the former, as is appropriate.

3.2 Politics and money

The reason why fees are as they are is due to politics as well as costs. Education is important to politicians and college education is especially so. Since 1999, the UK government has had an active policy to increase numbers of school-leavers who study at university. This has had a dramatic effect on all UK universities, who have seen increasing numbers of undergraduates each year.

Unfortunately, it has also had the side effect that most UK universities are getting short of money. Our universities are funded through government grants and students' fees. Neither is enough for many universities to operate as effectively as they would like. More students mean more costs in terms of equipment, lecturer salaries, facilities and support staff, and the costs rise faster than the increase in government support or student fees. This leads to compromises – perhaps the university focuses more on teaching and reduces its research efforts, or perhaps the teaching suffers while the research labs are improved. (Chapter 4 explains how to judge the university you are considering.)

In response, the UK government has also introduced an active policy to encourage more overseas students to UK universities. The government wishes the UK to have 25 per cent of the 'global market share' of fee-paying higher-education students. As you may have noticed, the language they use is more about money than education. In 1999, 'British exports of education and training' as the government phrases it, was worth £8 billion per year. That is a lot of extra cash to help out our universities.

This money cannot come from UK or EU students, because of yet another policy. This states that UK and EU students should have their fees subsidized – dramatically reduced compared to the actual costs – to encourage these students into further education. This is why a UK PhD student may only pay around £3000 per year, while an international PhD student may pay £13,000 per year. (Both would receive exactly the same tuition, equipment, use of facilities, and lab or office space.)

This may not seem terribly fair, but the universities would argue that the overseas tuition fees cover the actual costs, while the home fees are heavily subsidized. In reality, of course, this is not always true. It is very clear that universities are trying to increase the numbers of overseas students (encouraged by the government) in order to increase the amount of money raised to pay for all the other costs. Overseas students are thus an important source of revenue for universities.

You can use this information to your advantage – if you are an international student and are able to pay those large overseas fees, then it is extremely likely that you will be able to begin a doctorate in a UK university. It's not a nice thing to say, but it's true: money talks, and if you've got it, you'll be at a distinct advantage.

If you're from the UK or the EU, then you will only have to pay the smaller 'home fees'. Again, if you can prove that you will be able to pay these fees, you will find it much easier to begin your PhD. But remember that the university may be losing money with each home student they take on, so you will have to show them that you're capable of doing your doctorate quickly. It's in their interests to make UK and EU students complete their doctorates as quickly as possible. Indeed, some government funding councils will even reduce the amount of money they provide to departments for UK PhDs if they have students who take more than four years to finish. (Of course, it's also in the interests of the department to hold onto the overseas students for as long as possible so that they can keep receiving those huge fees, but you will never find anyone in a university who would admit this.)

These unfortunate politics and costs will also affect you if you have no money to pay the fees. Overseas fees cost so much, and the rules of eligibility for funding are so restrictive, that if you cannot get financial support from your own country, the chances of you being able to pay your fees may be dramatically reduced. Universities are no longer able to risk taking on students who may not be able to cope financially. Increasingly, students are not even being offered a place at a university if they cannot prove that their fees will be covered. However, one of the objectives of this book is to assist you with funding and fees, so don't despair. It may not be easy, but there are many options you can try to get funding and have all (or some) of your fees paid.

3.3   UK Research Councils

Funding for doctorates, and for UK research in general, comes from three different sources: the government, charities, and industrial sponsorship. Money from the government is of course always tied up with the politics of the party currently in power. The UK has a long history of university education and research excellence and so it is always a popular policy to encourage our ranking in the world. In 2004, 1.86 per cent of national income of the UK was invested in research and development. Over the following decade, the government has proposed to increase this to 2.5 per cent. The increase in government spending would put the UK more in line with European countries such as France (which spent 2.2 per cent of its national income on R&D in 2005), Germany (which spent 2.51 per cent) and the USA (which spent 2.67 per cent).

Even at 1.86 per cent, this still represents several billion pounds, which must be allocated to thousands of different research projects in hundreds of different fields. The money is handled by a series of complicated government departments such as the Office of Science and Technology (OST), (which helps allocate the UK science budget, currently just under £2.4 billion at the time of writing), part of the Department of Trade and Industry. The departments can change both in name and nature depending on the government. However, the majority of government money is now allocated by the Research Councils – government-funded bodies that have become so well established that they are unlikely to change in the near future.[7] There are eight Research Councils, each dedicated to funding a different type of research.

The Arts & Humanities Research Council (AHRC)

This is the newest of the councils to be created (prior to 2005 this was a 'Board' without the same powers as the other Research Councils). In addition to the change of name from AHRB to AHRC, the change to a council has meant that the AHRC is now more proscriptive about the type of research it wishes to fund, and it is introducing a new emphasis on the development of research skills for PhD students. This is leading to the introduction of new courses and schemes in some departments to enable their doctorate students to become competent at the kind of research described in Chapter 2.

The AHRC is divided into eight panels, each focused on a different area:

1   Classics, Ancient History and Archaeology;
2   Visual Arts and Media: practice, history, theory;
3   English Language and Literature;
4   Medieval and Modern History;
5   Modern Languages and Linguistics;
6   Librarianship, Information and Museum Studies;
7   Music and Performing Arts;
8   Philosophy, Law and Religious Studies.

Biotechnology and Biological Sciences Research Council (BBSRC)

The BBSRC was created in 1994 and is the main funder of basic and strategic biological research in the UK. It is divided into seven panels, which focus on different areas:

1   Agri-Food;
2   Animal Sciences;
3   Biochemistry and Cell Biology;
4   Biomolecular Sciences;
5   Engineering and Biological Systems;
6. Genes and Developmental Biology;
7. Plant and Microbial Sciences.

---

[7]   The facts and figures provided in this section come from the government report *'The Science and Innovation Investment Framework'* produced by the Treasury in 2004, and from material provided by the Research Councils, which is used with permission.

In addition, there are interdisciplinary areas that the BBSRC focuses on such as Bioinformatics, Biophysics, Bioscience Engineering, Cognitive Systems, Technology Development and Theoretical Biology.

Council for the Central Laboratory of the Research Councils (CCLRC)

The CCLRC supports the scientific facilities in the UK. It operates three world-class research laboratories: the Rutherford Appleton Laboratory in Oxfordshire, the Daresbury Laboratory in Cheshire and the Chilbolton Observatory in Hampshire. Together, the laboratories offer advanced facilities and expertise to support scientific research such as:

- ISIS, the world's most powerful pulsed neutron and muon source – used to study the atomic structure of materials;
- Synchrotron Radiation Source, the UK's brightest source of ultraviolet light and X-rays – for non-invasive research in materials and life sciences;
- The Central Laser Facility with high-power, state-of-the-art laser facilities for research in fundamental and applied science and engineering;
- Europe's largest Space Science and Technology department providing satellite-and ground-based instrumentation, testing and data analysis for Earth observation, astronomy and planetary science;
- Coordination and support of particle physics research in the UK and contribution to experiments at particle physics laboratories around the world including CERN;
- High capability computing using HPCx, one of Europe's most powerful academic research computers, e-Science, networking services and user support, and research in theoretical and computational science;
- Microelectronics facilities for the design, procurement, testing and commissioning of new devices and systems;
- World-leading wafer scale manufacturing processes for micro- and nano engineering;
- Research into alternative energy production, radio communications and radar.

On behalf of the UK government, the CCLRC is also the main shareholder in Diamond Light Source Limited. The Diamond synchrotron light source, the largest science facility to be built in the UK for more than 30 years, is due to start operations in 2007.

Economic & Social Research Council (ESRC)

The ESRC funds social science research – which they define as 'the study of society and the manner in which people behave and impact on the world around us'. The range of research funded by ESRC is extensive, as shown by their factsheets on the following areas:

- Economic performance and development;
- Environment and human behaviour;
- Governance and citizenship;
- Knowledge, communication and learning;
- Lifecourse, family and generations;
- Social stability and exclusion;
- Work and organization.

Engineering & Physical Sciences Research Council (EPSRC)

The EPSRC funds a broad range of subjects in engineering and the physical sciences, from mathematics to materials science, and from information technology to structural engineering. EPSRC currently focuses on ten areas:

1 Chemistry;
2 Engineering;
3 Information and Communication Technologies;
4 Infrastructure and Environment;
5 Innovative Manufacturing;
6 Life Sciences Interface;
7 Materials;
8 Mathematical Sciences;
9 Physics;
10 Public Engagement.

EPSRC does very well, receiving the highest amount of money from the Office of Science and Technology (as does the MRC). It also leads the way with schemes to encourage the public understanding of science.

Medical Research Council (MRC)

The MRC was established in 1913 and has a long and impressive history of achievements, from the discovery of the gene for Huntington's disease to the creation of the first DNA chip. The MRC focuses on six main areas of research:

1   People and Population Studies;
2   Neuroscience and Mental Health;
3   Immunology and Infection;
4   Genetics, Molecular Structure and Dynamics;
5   Cell Biology, Development and Growth;
6   Medical Physiology and Disease Processes.

Individual projects may also be funded under one of fourteen disease-specific divisions (or under the final, general division). These divisions cover the major common human health problems, as defined by impact on human health and healthcare cost, and significant areas of MRC research activity. The fifteenth division for unassigned research includes all research not directly related to a particular disease-specific research division, much of which is basic research. The divisions in 2005 were:

1   Cancer and Cell Proliferation;
2   Infections;
3   Neurological Disorders;
4   Circulatory Diseases;
5   Mental Health Disorders;
6   Reproductive Health;
7   Health of Elderly People;
8   Asthma and Other Respiratory Disorders;
9   Vision and Hearing;
10 Diabetes;
11 Arthritis and Rheumatism;
12 Oral Health;
13 Nutrition;
14 Children and Adolescents;
15 Other Diseases and Basic Research.

Natural Environment Research Council (NERC)

The Natural Environment Research Council funds independent research, surveys, training and knowledge transfer in the environmental sciences, to advance knowledge of our planet as a complex, interacting system. NERC covers a large range of atmospheric, earth, biological, terrestrial and aquatic sciences, from the deep oceans to the upper atmosphere, and from the poles to the equator. Some well-known research centres are wholly-owned, staffed and managed by NERC:

- British Antarctic Survey;
- British Geological Survey;
- Centre for Ecology and Hydrology;
- Proudman Oceanographic Laboratory.

NERC also funds collaborative centres by contract. These are managed from outside NERC and staff are not usually employed by NERC:

- National Oceanography Centre (in partnership with the University of Southampton);
- Centre for Observation and Modelling of Earthquakes and Tectonics;
- Centre of Observation of Air–Sea Interactions & Fluxes;
- Centre for Polar Observation & Modelling;
- Centre for Population Biology;
- Centre for Terrestrial Carbon Dynamics;
- Climate and Land Surface Systems Interaction Centre;
- Data Assimilation Research Centre;
- Environmental Systems Science Centre;
- NERC Centres for Atmospheric Science;
- National Institute for Environmental e-Science;
- Plymouth Marine Laboratory;
- Scottish Association for Marine Science;
- Sea Mammal Research Unit;
- Tyndall Centre.

Particle Physics and Astronomy Research Council (PPARC)

PPARC funds a programme of basic research in astronomy, space science and particle physics.[8] The council operates three scientific sites:

1   The UK Astronomy Technology Centre in Edinburgh;
2   The Isaac Newton Group in La Palma;
3   The Joint Astronomy Centre in Hawaii.

PARC funding is directed towards answering fundamental issues and supporting facilities identified in its science programme:

- Understanding of the fundamental particles of nature;
- Gravitational Waves to Cosmic Rays;
- Ground and Space-based facilities (e.g. the Visible Infrared Survey Telescope for Astronomy, due to start operations in Chile in 2006);
- Exploring our Solar System (e.g. SMART-1, a mission to test solar-electric propulsion manoeuvred into a near polar orbit of the moon in 2005);
- Grid Computing.

There is an increasing trend towards collaborative research, meaning that two or more councils may come together and jointly fund one project.

---

[8]   In the 2006 Budget, the government proposed that PPARC could be merged with EPSRC in the future.

These initially were set up as special schemes with names such as 'Basic Technology'. But more recently an umbrella body known as 'UKRC' (UK Research Councils) has been created to enable better interaction and collaboration between these large funding organizations. Nevertheless, most government-funded research is allocated by one Research Council at a time.

3.4   UK government funding

Hundreds of PhDs are funded by the Research Councils every year. Remember that this money comes from the UK government and so their eligibility rules apply – most government funding in the UK can only be awarded to UK or EU citizens (and EU citizens may only have their fees paid; they may not receive the additional bursary to live on). You will be eligible if you can demonstrate a relevant connection with the UK, usually through being ordinarily resident for a period of three years immediately prior to the date of application for an award (but not as a student). However, in 2005, a European Court of Justice ruling on a case brought by a French national modified this slightly – a non-UK, EU citizen resident in the UK for three or more years as a student is now eligible for full support (fees and bursary).

But it is more complicated. As a prospective PhD student, you are not eligible to apply to any of the research councils yourself. Normally, funding for doctorates is achieved in two ways: either a research council will provide a university department with a certain 'quota' of student funding, or a member of staff at a university must apply to the appropriate research council for the money.

The first method can be highly variable – quotas (or Doctoral Training Grants and Collaborative training accounts) are often allocated to departments based on measures of how successful that department is at helping students achieve their PhDs within four years. If too many students take too long, the quota may be cut back. Some universities have the newer 'Engineering Doctorate Centres', which currently receive a very healthy level of funding. However, these require a collaborating company to provide around £6,000 per year – not always easy for a member of staff at a university to arrange.

The second method – where a member of staff must apply for funding – is very different. Most research councils require that detailed proposals and complicated costings be produced. These are then sent to be reviewed by other experts in the area, then the proposal and its reviews are assessed by several judging committees. Sometimes the applicant must attend interviews or give presentations to a panel. This long process means that it can take anything from 2 to 12 months to prepare a proposal, and often 6 months before the result is given by the research councils. A 1-in-3 success rate is considered pretty good for these applications. There are some members of staff who never manage to get a single proposal accepted in their entire careers. But then there are others who know exactly which buzz-words to use to ensure that they keep bringing in the money, time and time again.

The exact process followed to apply for funding tends to vary according to the research area. It is not uncommon for Humanities students to write a research proposal with their potential supervisor, who then applies on behalf of the student. This will normally only happen if the supervisor knows the student already. One of the best ways to ensure your potential supervisor will apply for funding for you is to work with him or her during your MSc project. That way you get started on a research idea that can be developed into your doctorate, and you build a rapport with your supervisor.

In the sciences, it is more common for the supervisor to apply for money for a specific research project. If successful, the supervisor will be awarded funds to pay for research staff such as PhD students and also for equipment and travel costs. A funded PhD place is known as a *studentship* and may be open – in which case it is advertised like a job – or it may be named for a specific student. Because grants may be awarded at any time of year, there are always plenty of studentships being advertised, all the time. (The resources section at the end of the book describes where you can find adverts.) But do be aware if you apply for a studentship that your potential supervisor may have spent years trying to achieve funding for this idea. Don't apply for a studentship on a topic that you are not interested in just to get the money – the funding was provided for that research topic, so your supervisor really does want that topic to be investigated. Also be aware that many studentships are advertised badly. Some may give the impression that international students are eligible. This is almost never the case if the money comes from one of the UK research councils.

3.5   Overseas Research Students Awards Scheme and the Commonwealth Scholarship Commission

Government funding for PhDs can come from many different routes. If you are not eligible for funding from the UK research councils, don't worry. The first thing you should look at is the Overseas Research Students Award Scheme (also known as the ORSAS or ORS). The scheme was initiated in 1979 to attract high-quality international students to the United Kingdom to undertake research. Government funding is provided by the Department for Education and Skills (DfES) and is funded through four UK higher education funding bodies (for England, Scotland, Wales and Northern Ireland).

ORSAS awards provide funding to pay the difference between the international student tuition fees and the home student tuition fees charged by your university. So if your university is charging you £12,000 international fees per year and the home fees are £3,000, then your ORSAS grant will be £9,000 per year. ORSAS awards do not cover the home fee element, nor do they provide maintenance or travel expenses. The awards are paid directly to your university and used to pay part of your fees, so you will never actually see the money.

The scheme usually awards around 800 grants per year to students. A very healthy 65 per cent of applicants were successful in 2004, meaning that as long as you fill in the forms properly and have a good academic record, you have an excellent chance of obtaining this award. However, a word of warning. ORSAS has recently changed the way it operates. It now requires your university to make the initial decisions about which students should be given the awards. This may mean that if your university is popular or has a high percentage of international students, your chances of being successful may be much lower (you will be competing with many other students).

To apply for an ORSAS award, you must have been accepted at a university to begin your PhD. Your university will provide you with the application form. You will need to complete the form and give it back to your university (details and an example form are given in the resources section).

Another very useful source of funding is provided by the Commonwealth Scholarship Commission. This body was created in 1959 and was designed as a system of awards for men and women from all Commonwealth countries, chosen for their high intellectual promise and their ability to return and make a significant contribution to life in their own countries.

Funds for awards come from two government sources: the Foreign and Commonwealth Office, which provides an annual budget of around £2 million to support scholars from Canada, Australia and New Zealand; and the Department for International Development which provides an annual budget of some £10 million to support award holders from the remainder of the Commonwealth. To apply, you must obviously be a national of a Commonwealth country, and you must have a first-class academic record. These awards are difficult to obtain; competition is fierce. (More details are given in the resources section.)

3.6   Non-UK government funding

There are many different scholarships and funding options available to international students. It is very important that you examine all the options available to you – and check that you are eligible (normally eligibility is based on nationality and academic qualification). In addition to the Commonwealth Scholarship Commission mentioned above, there is also a body known as the Commonwealth Universities Study Abroad Consortium, which provides a small number of bursaries to Commonwealth students. American students should look at the Fulbright Scholarships and British Marshall Scholarships. Competition for all of these awards is fierce and deadlines can be a year before your proposed start date, so check early! Note that most UK universities will expect you to make the effort to find your own funding if you are an international student. You must check out your options and apply for these kinds of scholarships yourself – don't expect your university to do any work to help you. They usually won't. Go to the resources section for more details and links to websites where you can find the right funding programme for you.

Finally, the European Union has been funding research in its member countries for many years. The EU has a clear vision, in which it wishes to increase collaboration between countries, improve the sharing of resources, and enable researchers to exploit their expertise in several countries. Every few years a new framework programme is announced, which has specific research focuses and mechanisms for obtaining funding. Between 2002 and 2006, the Sixth Framework was active, focusing on areas such as:

- Life sciences, genomics and biotechnology for health;
- Information Society Technologies;
- Nanotechnologies and nanosciences;
- Aeronautics and space;
- Food quality and safety;
- Sustainable development, global change and ecosystems;
- Citizens and governance.

As the EU enlarges, the newer members are usually encouraged to participate in EU proposals. This means that proposals with collaborations that include countries such as Cyprus, the Czech Republic, Estonia, Hungary, Latvia, Lithuania, Malta, Poland, Slovakia and Slovenia are more likely to be successful.

EU proposals can be huge, with as many as twenty collaborating institutions each from a different country. They may be awarded many millions of Euros for their research, and some of the budget may well be allocated for PhD studentships. (There are also other smaller schemes designed to support researchers visiting new countries notably the Marie

Curie Research Training Networks.)[9] You cannot apply for money yourself – only members of staff at universities or in industry can apply for these grants. However, EU studentships do not have the same restrictions on eligibility as UK research council studentships. An EU (non-UK) citizen may have her fees paid but receive no bursary on an EPSRC grant; she may have the fees and a bursary on an EU grant. When applying for PhD studentships, find out where the money comes from – it may make a big difference.

3.7 Charities

In contrast to government money, the second source from which you can obtain funding is charities. Especially active in medical research, charities typically focus on a very specific issue or problem and will fund research that aims to tackle its area of interest. There are hundreds of charities in the UK alone. Table 3.1 lists those that are a member of the Association of Medical Research Charities (a membership organization of the leading UK charities that fund medical and health research). See the directory in the resources section at the end of the book for their webpages.

While the majority of charities do focus on medical research, some of the larger organizations such as the Wellcome Trust and the Leverhulme fund a broad range of research including mathematics, engineering and art. Even those that seem highly specialized (for example, the Ludwig Institute for Cancer Research) may collaborate with other university departments and fund studentships in computer analysis, data mining or mathematical modelling.

Funding can be obtaining from many different routes, depending on the charity. Some offer prize studentships for which you can apply directly. Others require your supervisors to apply for studentships in much the same way as they would apply for money from the Research Councils (details of how and when to apply are given in the resources section). One distinct advantage of many charities is that they can make their decisions much faster than the councils. The disadvantage is that they have much less money available.

---

[9] See this website for more details: http://europa.eu.int/comm/research/fp6/mariecurie-actions/pdf/rtn_hand.pdf

Table 3.1 Members of the Association of Medical Research Charities
http://www.amrc.org.uk/

Action Cancer	Action Medical Research	Action on Addiction	Alzheimer's Research Trust
Alzheimer's Society	Arthritis Research Campaign	Association for International Cancer Research	Association for Spina Bifida and Hydrocephalus (ASBAH)
Asthma UK	Ataxia	Ataxia-Telangiectasia Society	BackCare
Barnwood House Trust	Blackie Foundation Trust	Brain Research Trust	Breakthrough Breast Cancer
Breast Cancer Campaign	British Council for Prevention of Blindness	British Eye Research Foundation	British Heart Foundation
British Liver Trust	British Lung Foundation	British Occupational Health Research Foundation	British Retinitis Pigmentosa Society
British Sjögren's Syndrome Association	British Skin Foundation	British Vascular Foundation	BUPA Foundation
Cancer Research UK	CFS Research Foundation	Chest Heart And Stroke Scotland	Children's Liver Disease Foundation
Chronic Disease Research Foundation	Chronic Granulomatous Disorder Research Trust	Cystic Fibrosis Trust	Defeating Deafness (aka Hearing Research Trust)
Diabetes Research and Wellness Foundation	Diabetes UK	Digestive Disorders Foundation	Dystrophic Epidermolysis Bullosa Research Association (DEBRA)
Epilepsy Research Foundation	Foundation for Liver Research	Foundation for the Study of Infant Deaths	Fund for Epilepsy
Guy's and St Thomas' Charity	Health Foundation (formerly PPP Foundation)	Heart Research UK	Huntington's Disease Association
Hypertension Trust	Inspire Foundation (aka Integrated Spinal Rehabilitation Foundation)	International Spinal Research Trust	Juvenile Diabetes Research Foundation UK
Lister Institute of Preventive Medicine	Ludwig Institute for Cancer Research	Marie Curie Research Institute	Meningitis Research Foundation

Meningitis Trust	Migraine Trust	Motor Neurone Disease Association	Multiple Sclerosis Society of Great Britain and Northern Ireland
Muscular Dystrophy Campaign	Myasthenia Gravis Association	National Association for Colitis and Crohn's Disease	National Eczema Society
National Endometriosis Society	National Eye Research Centre	National Kidney Research Fund	National Osteoporosis Society
Neuro-Disability Research Trust	North West Cancer Research Fund	Northern Ireland Chest Heart and Stroke Association	Northern Ireland Leukaemia Research Fund
Novartis Foundation	Novo Nordisk UK Research Foundation	Nuffield Foundation	Parkinson's Disease Society of the UK
PBC Foundation	Primary Immunodeficiency Association	Progressive Supranuclear Palsy Association	Psoriasis Association
Queen Victoria Hospital Blond McIndoe Research Foundation	RAFT (Restoration of Appearance and Function Trust)	Remedi	Research into Ageing
Royal College of Radiologists	Royal College of Surgeons of England	St Peter's Trust for Kidney, Bladder & Prostate Research	Scottish Hospital Endowments Research Trust
Sir Jules Thorn Charitable Trust	Society For Endocrinology	Sparks (Sport Aiding Medical Research for Kids)	Spencer Dayman Meningitis UK
Stroke Association	Tenovus	Tommy's The Baby Charity	Tuberous Sclerosis Association
Tyneside Leukaemia Research Association	Ulster Cancer Foundation	Wellbeing	WellChild
Wellcome Trust	Wessex Medical Trust (aka Hope)	World Cancer Research Fund	Yorkshire Cancer Research

Another advantage of obtaining funding from charities is that the eligibility requirements are set by the charity, not by the UK government, so international students can be funded. Nevertheless, few charities want to spend £13,000 a year on international fees when they can spend just £3,000 on a home student. The money comes from hard-won donations and they cannot afford to waste it. This means an international student should apply for an ORSAS grant to reduce the fees to the home student level and then approach (or have their supervisor contact) a charity.

3.8   Industry

Industrial funding can be a very effective way of paying for a PhD, and there are several old and new schemes where companies can pay for part of the costs, with the government providing the rest. One such scheme is the CASE studentship. CASE studentships are 3½-year awards allocated to companies and other bodies (such as Faraday Partnerships and Regional Development Agencies). They enable companies to take the lead in defining and arranging projects with an academic partner of their choice. The company provides a substantial financial contribution to the project and the student must spend at least three months during the period of the award at their premises – although some companies host the students for almost the entire duration.

It is up to the company to do the work. They must approach a research council and ask for a CASE award allocation. These allocations are based on previous collaborations by the company with research projects – more collaborations mean more CASE awards. Usually only the larger companies (for example, BAE Systems, BT) can afford the financial costs, provide the space and spare the time for collaborations to enable them to receive large allocations. But it is in their interests to get involved – a CASE studentship costs them far less than paying a full-time research engineer. There are provisions for smaller companies to become involved as well, with less financial burden.

Once the company has been allocated a studentship, they must find an academic partner to enable those students to be registered for a doctorate. Again, the choice of university is up to the company. The CASE studentship is then advertised in the same manner as an ordinary studentship, and you will be able to apply for it as normal.

There are other variations of the CASE, such as the TCS (teaching company scheme) which can be used to fund students, or the EngD, which is a new form of doctorate available from some Engineering Doctorate Centres in certain universities.[10] The EngD resembles an American PhD – the first year or two has a taught element, often including group projects, management and business skills, in addition to subject-specific courses. Engineering doctorate students may be expected to spend most of their time at a collaborating company (which will pay around £6,000 a year to the university). Unlike the CASE studentships, EngDs are managed by the host university and it is the responsibility of the university to find a

---

[10]   The Engineering Doctorate Scheme, launched in 1992, has now established itself as EPSRC's flagship qualification. At the time of writing, a review was being performed to ensure it continued to be relevant to its key stakeholders in academia and industry. The review may result in new recommendations and changes to be made to the way the scheme is managed and advertised in the future, so check all details of the course you are interested in.

company prepared to collaborate. This can sometimes be a challenge, especially since most companies require contracts and Intellectual Property Rights agreements to be drawn up. Sometimes the paperwork can take almost as long as the doctorate to complete as the university goes through protracted negotiations with the company – but luckily this does not prevent EngD students from starting when they want to. The New Route PhD™ is a cross between a PhD and EngD – there is no requirement for a collaborating company, but the scheme is four years and has a similar taught element. New Route PhD™ scholarships are being offered at a number of participating universities – you should contact individual universities for full details (the list of universities is given in the resources section).

The final type of industrial sponsorship is the rarest – a rich company simply sponsors a student for the duration of their PhD. Some companies are able to write off these 'trivial' expenses for tax purposes and so £20,000 a year may be very easy for them to find. As you might expect, usually the best way to arrange a deal like this is to talk with the owner or president of the company – something that well-placed staff at a university can do, now and again.

Whatever the form of industrial support, you should be aware that it is quite a different form of funding. Obviously, companies exist to make money. While it is possible that some of the larger and richer companies can sometimes afford to fund blue-sky research now and again, generally most companies will want to see some practical and useful result from you. This means that most industrial sponsorship is for very applied research, which has a high potential to become a product in the near future. Your sponsors also may want to keep tight control over what you do, and may prevent you from publishing anything, to avoid giving their competition any ideas. You must weigh the academic constraints against the benefits. You will find it much harder to do pure research and build a reputation as an academic researcher with this form of funding. But you are considerably more likely to achieve patents, do practical and useful work, and be employed by your sponsors at the end. (You are also more likely to get a decent-sized bursary with industrial sponsorship – usually they are the largest of all forms of funding.) If you see your future as an academic in a university, then you may not be happy with industrial sponsorship, but if you see yourself working in industry, then it could be ideal for you.

3.9 How to apply

A PhD is an expensive degree and few students can afford to fund themselves. Those that try often find that they are heavily in debt by the end. It is safer to assume that you will need some kind of funding and apply for it at the very beginning. In subsequent chapters, this book describes how to choose a university, supervisor and write a research proposal, before applying for your PhD place and corresponding funding. You are recommended to follow these steps – unless you apply for an advertised studentship, in which case you have no choice about the university, supervisor or project, but the funding is already sorted out. (Nevertheless you should still visit the supervisor and check everything out, for you always have the choice of not accepting the studentship.)

The previous sections described your various choices for funding and where that money might come from. This final section summarizes your options. You have many choices of how to apply for a PhD and relevant funding. In the UK, these are determined by your nationality, your academic qualifications, and you. If you are an EU or UK citizen, then you have eight options.

1   Apply to universities for funded places

If you are a UK citizen or an EU citizen who has spent three years or more in the UK (to demonstrate residency) then you will be eligible to apply for the small number of funded places that some departments are given each year by the UK research councils. If a department has several places available, it may advertise (in the same places as studentships), often listing a series of general topics that are of interest, and supervisors that are willing to take on students. Don't be confused if some adverts call these places 'studentships' – the money comes in the form of quotas to the department (in contrast to PhD studentships which are funded as part of specific research projects with specific supervisors, see below). You can tell if the advertised place is a quota place because it will ask you to suggest a research project, and will usually suggest a starting date of September or October. Competition may be as fierce as 50 applicants for each place, so you will typically need the equivalent of a first-class degree and distinction in a Masters degree, as well as an outstanding application and research proposal to be successful. You are unlikely to be chosen without the support of your potential supervisor. (It is often very useful if the supervisor supervised you for your MSc or undergraduate project.) Most universities make their decisions about these funded places in the summer and expect the students to start in the autumn, so you should make enquiries in the first few months of the year and ensure you have applied for the place by May.

2   Apply to universities for advertised studentships

Studentships are advertised all the year round and provide the easiest and safest way to obtain a funded PhD place. (The resources section provides details of where to look.) Competition may be fierce, but this will depend on the project, the area of research, the university and the time of year – sometimes there may be a hundred applicants for one position; sometimes the university has to readvertise because they have not received any applications from suitable candidates. If the studentship is funded by the UK research councils, you will be eligible for the full award (fees and maintenance grant) if you are a UK citizen or resident in the UK (there are strict rules about how this is defined, see Section 3.3). If you are an EU citizen you may be eligible only to have your fees paid. If you are an international student, you may not be eligible for any money. If the studentship is funded by the EU, then EU citizens will be eligible for the full amount; various rules apply for international students. To be successful, you must demonstrate academic qualifications, interest and ideally some experience in the area of the studentship. Meeting the supervisor and discussing the research is always a good idea.

3   Apply to universities for New Route PhDs™

New Route PhDs™ are only available at certain participating universities (see the resources section). The eligibility rules are much the same as for advertised studentships (see above). This is a very new scheme and so competition is a little less for these positions. New Route PhDs™ have a significant taught component, so in addition to defining your research interests you will have to choose which courses to take. Meeting a potential supervisor and the director of the New Route PhD™ scheme is advisable. These doctorates always begin at the start of the new academic year, so deadlines for applications are several months prior to this. If you wish to undertake a 'Split PhD' then you will also have to find another university or institute prepared to collaborate with the New Route PhD™ university, and another supervisor prepared to support you.

4   Find a collaborating company and apply to a university for an EngD

The Engineering Doctorate is another scheme involving a significant taught component, and thus students begin in September/October and must apply several months before this. The EngD is only available at a few centres at specific universities in the country (see the resources section). There are usually several places available every year at each centre, and because of the requirement to find a collaborating company (which must provide you with office space and £6,000 per year), these places may not all be filled each year. To be successful, you must satisfy the same eligibility requirements as described for advertised studentships, and ideally find or help to find the collaborating company. Some supervisors can assist if you approach them, but it is always hard to convince a company to support academic research. A second option available for EngDs is for employees of a company to remain at their place of work and register for the EngD at the same time. Such EngD students may not receive the full grant and the company will be required to provide sufficient time for the student to perform research and attend courses at the university.

5   Apply for an advertised CASE studentship

CASE studentships are advertised in the same places as normal PhD studentships. It is common for CASE PhD students to perform their research at the company that receives the funding, so applicants are typically expected to have practical experience relevant to the advertised project in addition to academic qualifications. The same eligibility rules apply, except that some companies may perform their own, additional vetting procedure (you may be required to satisfy other eligibility requirements if a security clearance is needed, for example). CASE studentships are often very practical, and often lead to full-time employment after the end of the doctorate, so competition can be intense. These studentships may be advertised at various times of the year, but most quotas are allocated annually to companies by the UK research councils. Companies normally have a very precise idea of the research they would like to be performed, so you may not be able to alter the scope or topic of your doctorate.

6   Apply for a PhD place and then apply for charity funding

If you attempt the first option in this list and do not receive funding from the department, then you may still have a PhD place at the university, which is conditional on you paying the fees. One option you can then take is to accept the place, and then apply for funding from a charity to pay your fees (and hopefully some of your bills as well). Some charities offer their own scholarships to provide full funding for PhDs performing research in their area of interest. If you know that your research may be relevant to charities, it is worth applying to one or more (in some cases your supervisor might have to apply on your behalf). The resources section provides some examples of scholarships available annually from some charities. These will often be advertised, although sometimes only on publications or websites specific to that form of research. Charities do not have much money and obviously want to ensure that their hard-won donations are spent on the very best and most useful research. It is normally sensible to enlist the help of your supervisor to keep the research relevant. The amount of awards may vary and eligibility requirements vary also.

---

7   Apply for a PhD place and arrange for full sponsorship from a company

If you try the first option in this list and receive a conditional place but no funding, then you can accept the place and obtain funding from a company. This is not an easy option, for the research must clearly be relevant to the company involved, and it is very difficult to persuade industry to spend money without seeing a clear return. Nevertheless, some fast-talking supervisors (or PhD students themselves) are able to convince managing directors that funding a PhD student is a cheap way of getting some key research done. There are no eligibility requirements for this kind of funding; it is down to you or your supervisor to negotiate a deal. If you are prepared to allow the company to own your findings or products of your research, then they may regard this as a good deal.

---

8   Apply for a PhD place and pay for everything from savings or with help from family

If you attempt all other options in this list and only manage to secure an unfunded conditional PhD position, then your last resort should be to pay the fees yourself. Savings, loans or family will certainly cover your costs in the short term, but you should never stop looking for funding. Eventually you will find the financial burden too distracting, so this should not be considered a final solution.

If you are not from the UK or EU, and you cannot demonstrate residency in the UK then you have two other options.

---

9   Apply for a PhD place and then apply for ORSAS funding in combination with 1 to 8 above (where permitted)

As an international student, you are probably not eligible for quota places in universities (paid for by the UK research councils). Instead, you should apply for a PhD place and also apply for ORSAS funding. This will not cover all of your costs, it simply reduces the international fees to the same as home fees, which then need to be paid. In combination with ORSAS, you should explore the other forms of funding listed above. You may not be eligible for options 1 to 5, however, don't just assume this is true without checking. In rare cases, a quota place in a department is funded using the department's money and not the cash from UK research council, meaning that they are free to spend the cash on you. Sometimes an advertised studentship is funded from a different source, meaning that you are eligible. If you can get an ORSAS grant, you will cost no more than a UK or EU student, so this immediately improves your chances of getting further funding. (The resources section explains exactly how to apply for ORSAS.)

---

10   Apply for a PhD place and apply for a scholarship from your country or from the British Council

---

Restrictions for funding international students are severe in the UK, so many, many schemes have been introduced to try to overcome these issues. There are now scholarships specifically for Americans, Commonwealth nationals, Far East nationals, and indeed most nationalities, to fund them to study PhDs in the UK. Eligibility for these scholarships is extremely variable and extremely strict – you normally must be the right nationality to qualify and you typically need to demonstrate outstanding academic achievement to stand a chance of being successful. Nevertheless, there are so many different schemes that you will probably be eligible for two or three. The deadlines for some scholarships are nearly a year in advance and you may often have to apply in your own country. Some are designed to be used with an ORSAS grant, others do not permit this. The resources section at the back of the book provides details of some of the scholarships available, and where to look to find more.

4

Finding the right university

Whether you are applying for a studentship or trying to find funding yourself, you need to pick the university you wish to go to. You will typically be able to choose between several options as you discover studentships, or as you make contact with friendly supervisors at different universities (see Chapter 5). But in order to finalize your funding or supervisor, you will have to make an important decision: which university is best for you?

The problem is that there are so many different ways of judging a university, and you can be sure that each university has figured out what it's best at and will promote that aspect, while sweeping all of its bad points under the carpet. So how do you choose? Is a famous, old university better than a young, trendy one? Is a department that receives a lot of coverage on television better than one that receives a lot of respect from the scientific community? Is a university in a big city better than one in a large park in the country? Is the amount of money the department receives more important than the number of scientific publications it produces? Does a good research rating but a poor record for teaching mean that it will be a better or worse place for your research?

Luckily, because a PhD is mostly a personal activity that does not rely on the quality of lecturers or equipment, and because they are assessed by external examiners, all PhDs are pretty much equal, regardless of where you do your doctorate. There is much less snobbery about PhDs than for other degrees. But sadly, some of those based in the older institutions or bodies (such as Oxford or the Royal Institution) will still be biased against

Table 4.1 Some of the oldest universities in the UK

University	Founded
University of Oxford	between 1096 and 1167
University of Cambridge	1209
University of St Andrews	1413
University of Glasgow	1451
University of Aberdeen	1495
University College London	1826
University of Durham	1837

you if you 'make the mistake' of going to the wrong university. Nevertheless, you should consider that attitude to be their problem, not yours.

4.1 Old or new?

Before you can make an informed choice, it is important you know the history of universities in the UK. Oxbridge (Oxford and Cambridge) are proud to be the 'oldest universities in the English-speaking world'. But there are many historic universities in the UK that date back several centuries, see Table 4.1.

Age typically equates to prestige in universities. The older the university, the more chance it has had for some famous people to be educated there, and the more chance for its graduates to reach positions of power to help their old university. The oldest universities are rich in tradition (and often in money as well), often making them comfortable and career-enhancing places to go.

Things began to change after the 1850s when the so-called 'ancient universities' were joined by a new crop of 'red brick' universities.[11] These civic universities owed their heritage in part to the freedoms introduced by University College London, for they admitted both men and women and required no religious assent.[12] Table 4.2 lists the six civic universities created around this time.

---

[11] The term 'Red Brick' was first coined by a professor of music at the University of Liverpool to describe these civic universities. His reference was inspired by the fact that the Victoria Building at the University of Liverpool (which was designed by Alfred Waterhouse and completed in 1892) is built from a distinctive red pressed brick, with terracotta decorative dressings.

[12] Oxbridge and Durham required their students to satisfy religious tests; specifically, assent to the Thirty-Nine Articles, the defining statements of Anglican doctrine.

Table 4.2 The red brick universities (Most have origins that date back considerably earlier than the years listed.)

University	Founded
University of Birmingham	1900
University of Bristol	1909
University of Leeds	1904
University of Liverpool	1903
University of Manchester	1903
University of Sheffield	1905

There are several other universities that also formed around this time and are occasionally referred to as 'red brick', such as the University of Reading, which split from Oxford and became a university in its own right in 1926, and Queen's University, Belfast, which was created when the Royal University of Ireland was disbanded in the Irish Universities Act, 1908. Other examples include the University of Exeter, which split from Cambridge in 1955, the University of Newcastle Upon Tyne, which split from Durham in 1963, the University of Nottingham, which split from the University of London in 1948 and the University of Southampton, which split from the University of London in 1952. (It is normally considered insulting to refer to UCL as red brick, however.)

In the meantime, from 1836, several separate London-based colleges (such as UCL, King's, Imperial, Queen Mary, Royal Holloway, Goldsmiths, and the School of African and Oriental Studies) grew and merged to form the University of London. Today, this is a vast federation of colleges and institutes, whose constituents act as independent universities (and often compete with some rivalry). Some are Recognized Bodies (meaning they have the authority to grant their own degrees like truly separate universities). Others are Listed Bodies that must award degrees through the University of London, like the colleges of Oxford, Cambridge and Durham.

The next important change to UK universities came following a government report known as the Robbins Report, in 1963. This recommended an immediate expansion of the university system in the UK and led to the creation of several new universities. These became known as the glass plate universities, in contrast to the red brick ones. At the time they were built, concrete and glass were very much in vogue, so most glass plate universities are very distinctive in design (and some are just plain ugly). Table 4.3 lists the glass plate universities.

In addition to looking distinctive, many glass plate universities are campus universities, often built like little towns in their own right, with shops, banks, student accommodation and university buildings all together on one site. Some are based in very pretty settings, for example, the University of Essex, based in Wivenhoe Park. These universities are not

Table 4.3 Some of the glass plate universities (Several have origins that date back considerably earlier than the years listed.)

University	Founded
Brunel University	1966
Heriot-Watt University	1966
University of Bath	1966
University of Bradford	1966
University of East Anglia	1963
University of Essex	1965
University of Kent	1965
Keele University	1962
University of Lancaster	1964
Loughborough University	1966
University of Stirling	1967
University of Sussex	1961
University of Surrey	1966
University of Warwick	1965
New University of Ulster	1968
University of York	1963

collegiate (comprising of separate colleges), like Cambridge, but they may be spread across several campuses as separate institutes merge into one university.

The Open University was also granted its Royal Charter at around this time (1969), although its history dates from ideas by Harold Wilson (the Prime Minister at the time) to create a 'university of the air' to provide a university education for all. Now based in Milton Keynes, it still leads the way with innovative distance teaching methods through national television and radio programmes and has several full-time and part-time PhD schemes that are designed to encourage a broad range of students from all backgrounds.

Although these universities are still sometimes referred to as the 'new universities', in 1992 the final and perhaps most dramatic change occurred to the UK university system, which created many more, even newer ones. Before that date there were two very distinct types of higher education establishment: the university (as described above), and the polytechnic. In the UK, polytechnics are institutes dedicated mainly to vocational studies (akin to the tradition of apprenticeships, these are courses designed to equip practical students with skills needed in the workplace rather than pure academic qualifications).

In 1992, the government introduced the 'Further and Higher Education Act', which altered the funding and administration of institutes and enabled polytechnics to be converted into full universities, with the power

Table 4.4 Some of the post-1992 universities in the UK

Abertay University	Anglia Polytechnic University	University of Brighton	Bournemouth University
University of Central England	University of Central Lancashire	Coventry University	University of Derby
De Montfort University	University of East London	University of Glamorgan	Glasgow Caledonian University
University of Greenwich	University of Hertfordshire	University of Huddersfield	Kingston University
Leeds Metropolitan University	University of Lincoln	Liverpool John Moores University	London Guildhall University (now part of London Metropolitan University)
University of Luton	Manchester Metropolitan University	Middlesex University	Napier University
University of North London (now part of London Metropolitan University)	University of Northumbria	Nottingham Trent University	Oxford Brookes University
University of Paisley	University of Plymouth	University of Portsmouth	Sheffield Hallam University
South Bank University	Staffordshire University	University of Sunderland	University of Teesside
Thames Valley University	Robert Gordon University	University of the West of England	University of Westminster
University of Wolverhampton			

to grant their own degrees, including PhDs. This resulted in the creation of many new (or 'modern', or post-1992) universities (see Table 4.4).

Until recently, these new universities were not regarded as being of the same quality as the glass plate, red brick or ancient universities described so far. The stigma of 'vocational learning' has stuck with many, resulting in a perception of lower academic quality. While the research facilities of some post-1992 universities did need improving, the strong background most had in teaching means that in reality many are very good in education. Perceptions are now beginning to change rapidly as the number of students increase, and the older universities are struggling to keep up. Some of the post-1992 universities are showing their flair and dynamism as they create modern courses, build brand new facilities and attract many new students. Some of the older universities are heavily in debt, their facilities are decaying and their administration sucks up vast amounts of money.

Nevertheless, there are still some entrenched biases in UK universities. The more prestigious universities (the older ones) still have higher entry requirements for their students. They also receive far more applications for all their student places, including the PhD places, so competition is much more fierce. This means that, regardless of the true quality of research, the older universities often end up with the better PhD candidates. It is not necessarily fair or sensible, but that is the way it is.

4.2 Where?

Whether you are considering an ancient, red brick, glass plate or post-1992 university, there are some important considerations. Perhaps the most basic of these is: do you want to live in the town where the university is based? If you are a city person, you may find a move to a campus-based university is unbearably dreary. If you are a country person, a bustling central university may be much too stressful. Remember that the average PhD takes four years. Are you sure you can live in that town for four years?

The different regions of the UK are very distinct, with strong accent and speech differences. We are all capable of learning how to hear sounds we're not used to, in time, but if your native language is sufficiently different from English you may find some regional accents very challenging to understand. At the very least, you need to ensure that you can communicate with your supervisor without difficulty. It can be a terribly lonely experience to find yourself surrounded by strangers who speak in a way you find hard to follow.

Some international students are tempted to go to a university in a big city, where there will almost certainly be a community of others from your country, and even supermarkets selling familiar foods, and bookstores selling familiar books. You will certainly find this much easier, but there is a real danger that you will not integrate properly and your English language skills may not improve. One of my students (from Korea) found that a good approach for international students is to do a Masters degree at a university in a smaller town, where you will be forced to learn the English language quickly and well, and then do your PhD in a larger town where you will have the support of a community of others like you.

There are also subtle cultural differences across the UK. In the south, people tend to be more health-conscious and cosmopolitan. In the north, people may be friendlier and less pretentious. In the cities, there is usually much greater diversity of cultures than in the country, but then crime and ghettos are also more common. These differences even affect living costs. Everything is more expensive in the south, and in the cities.

It is not sensible to generalize about people or culture – there are always rough areas in any town that you'd be wise to avoid, and there are always nice regions that you'd probably be safe and comfortable in. Luckily the Internet is so good that you should be able to do a basic search on news stories or statistics for any town to give yourself a better idea of the prosperity and diversity of its regions. You should even be able to find costs of accommodation online to give yourself an idea of how much it will cost to live there (see Chapter 8 for more about accommodation). Of course, the best thing you can do is visit the university and its region.

The next chapter (Chapter 5) explains how to get in touch with potential supervisors. When you go and talk with them (or when you go for an interview for a studentship), it is very important that you take the opportunity to look around the university and the region. Try to get someone (ideally your potential supervisor) to give you a tour. There are several important things you need to check out: the university buildings, the PhD facilities, typical student accommodation, and the support staff.

My own experience at the start of my PhD was not terribly positive. I had been awarded a studentship, and a week before I was due to move up there, my supervisor rang me to tell me that my department's building had just been condemned by building inspectors. Because of safety reasons, they were recommending that it should be demolished. Suddenly my dreams of doing a PhD were thrown into turmoil – if my new university was falling apart before I arrived, what would it be like when I got there?

It worked out OK in the end for me (they bolted the building together for a few more years while they built brand new facilities). But do be aware that the prosperity of universities can be very different. Regardless of its age, location, fame, or the fees you pay, a university may have wonderful, clean and modern facilities, or it may be using buildings that have leaking roofs, wobbly tables and mouldy walls. If your PhD requires you to work in a lab or office, it is important that you go and see exactly what you will be getting. The chances are high that a poor department won't have anything terribly nice for you.

It is also worth walking around the region where the university is situated. Because the government tries to regenerate some of the poorer parts of towns, you sometimes find that a university has been built next to a rather undesirable place to live. It is important to take a look for yourself and to ask the existing students for their experiences.

Finally, when you visit the university, try to meet some of the other staff who are there to help you. Try to gauge the atmosphere of the place by talking by them. There may be other members of the research group, and there will be various secretaries, technicians and student advisors. You will get to meet many of these at your interview. Scowling, grumpy researchers, and administrators who snap may be a sign that people in the department are feeling stressed and unhappy. Generally, a happy department will have helpful and pleasant staff who are able to help students with their problems.

4.3   Do they do what you're interested in?

Nobody really decides which university to go to based solely on where it is or how old it is (or if they do, they're very foolish). The most important thing you need to know about your university is how well they can support your PhD work. You cannot do research without help. Even the best PhD student in the world needs guidance on what they need to do to produce a thesis worthy of a doctorate. Most of us also need help with many other aspects along the way: how to write and present a conference paper, how to critically review the work of others, how to analyse a problem, run experiments, and derive meaning from results. It is also important to have someone who will challenge you, forcing you to defend your ideas (or update them).

A good research environment will provide all of these needs. Your supervisor may provide much of your support, but a department where your research is respected and understood, or group full of people who have similar interests will provide you with a much more stimulating environment than one in which you work alone as a misunderstood outsider. In a good department you'll be able to take part in seminar series or group discussions to help you learn key presentation and defence skills. You will also have many more people to ask for help should your supervisor be unavailable or lacking in knowledge in a certain area.

It is usually very easy to ascertain the research interests of a department. Today, every university maintains detailed web pages on the research of every member of staff. The more successful staff will arrange themselves into clear research groups that have an obvious focus. Most research groups also have web pages, which describe the work, its members, lists of publications and so on. The best of these research groups will quickly become quite famous in their own right, with many links from other people's pages. When you are looking for a good place to go (and a good potential supervisor), some basic Internet searching should quickly identify the larger and better groups.

It is less important to find a group if you're interested in a PhD in the humanities, where you're more likely to be working on your own, away from the department for large amounts of time. But in the sciences it is often imperative to find a group that contains the right mix of experts and the right facilities for your research. These will be clearly advertised by the group or department. Famous people often get a mention and a specialized and unique form of equipment, such as a microscope, or particle accelerator, or radio telescope, is often a very significant asset for a department. Even just having modern and well-equipped labs can make an enormous difference – perhaps reducing the time needed for your experiments by years. Clearly you need to ensure that you find a university that will enable you to work most efficiently and effectively.

Successful groups are often led by one or more (potentially famous) professors who have successfully obtained lots of funding to pay for equipment and staff. But note that not all professors are able to achieve this. The capabilities of staff may be related to the quality of the university. As we saw earlier, the older universities (and especially the ancient universities) are considered more prestigious than the newer post-1992 universities. This does mean that you are more likely to find world-class groups and very famous researchers in the older universities – simply because those universities can afford to headhunt the best people and offer them more money and better facilities. There is also a bias for these universities to receive more funding – they are already associated with quality so they have less to prove to the funders. There are always exceptions, however. A young ambitious academic will often first become a professor in a slightly less prestigious university (where there is more freedom and less competition). And some post-1992 universities are now becoming just as rich as the older universities, while some older universities are in debt and need to downsize – so good people and great research groups can be found almost anywhere.

4.4   Research cultures

The way research is performed and the way in which it is supported differ for subject area and university. You may not always have much choice in the matter, but it is important to be aware of the differences. For example, in many biological sciences, PhD students may be expected to maintain and run specific equipment, work as part of a team, and to follow their supervisors' research plan quite strictly. Biological funding is often carefully targeted towards supporting specific research goals and equipment, and you may not be able to change the course of your research easily. But you will gain from working as part of a team, and may have day-to-day support from your supervisor and fellow researchers.

Contrast this with the humanities where PhD students may be given almost complete autonomy and may be left on their own to follow their personal research ideas. There might be no interaction within a larger group and very infrequent meetings with your supervisor. It's not all bad news – you have considerably more freedom to follow your own ideas – but you might find the lack of support makes your doctorate a lonely business.

The variation in research culture that you experience will also differ according to individual supervisors' views within departments. Some supervisors are very 'hands off' – they expect you to get on with your own work and may only see you at infrequent pre-arranged appointment times. Others are the opposite – they may have their office integrated into the lab and you may see and work with them daily. Some supervisors believe they should be authoritative and act like an aloof General; others prefer a friendly team and socialize with their students outside work. (See Chapter 5 for more details about supervisors.) The only way you can figure out what your supervisor is going to be like is by talking with them and with their existing students.

You will also find that there are subtle differences in universities that make a difference to student life. For example, many city universities have to lock their doors by 7 p.m. to reduce the chances of crime. This can prevent the kind of late-night research communities that grow and socialize together in universities that stay open all the time. There can also be considerable variation in how staff and students interact – often caused as much by the design of the department buildings than by anything else. A department with offices that surround a shared open-plan or social area will usually have much more interaction than one that has offices all leading from narrow corridors with an isolated social area in the middle of nowhere. A department with shared common rooms for staff and students will produce a much more sociable environment than one that segregates everyone according to their position. One of the nicest research environments I've seen is at the Sante Fe Institute, USA, where all the staff offices surround open-plan research areas, with the added benefit of open-air courtyards, a big kitchen designed to feel like a homely farmhouse kitchen and regular times for coffee breaks and lunches during which everyone gets together for good conversation. Sadly, this kind of arrangement is an exception rather than the norm. The internal architecture of most UK universities is based on claustrophobic corridors, and privacy and isolation rather than integration, which is a shame.

Some universities have policies designed to integrate PhD students better. Departments may have reading groups or seminar series in which PhD students are required to participate. Reading groups generally comprise a number of research students and staff who come together to discuss key research papers each week (sometimes authored by a member of the group). A good reading group will have heated debate and cutting criticism of the current paper, enabling students to gain experience of critical review and defence. In some universities, the reading group may be run by the students themselves and funding may be provided to enable them to invite well-known speakers now and again. Student seminar series are common and many universities require every PhD student to present their work to their department at least once during their PhD. This helps provide the kind of experience that will later be needed for presenting conference papers. Universities may also require supervisors to see their students regularly (with reports that must be filled in to guarantee this).

Themes of student integration can be taken further in many institutions, with PhD students being allowed to give tutorials, do lab demonstration work and even supervise undergraduate projects. (You are usually paid for any teaching that you do.) In some universities (such as Cambridge) this is taken even further, with the culture of PhD tutors, where each PhD student is expected to tutor two undergraduate students, assisting them with coursework and general skills. Such schemes are designed to help you be an important part of the university, while enabling undergraduate students to learn from the cutting-edge research that students like you are doing.

Even if your university does not have such a culture, you will find that you have a lot of freedom to help mould your environment to the way you like it. If there are no reading groups, don't be afraid of setting one up yourself. If you would like to interact more with undergraduates, why not look into lab demonstrating or project supervision? If you'd prefer to interact socially, all universities have student unions and student clubs, so you can always take part in student life whether you're into juggling, flying, rowing or social drinking. There are a few differences in the types of clubs available at each university, but once again, if there's not one for the activity you prefer, there's usually nothing to stop you from going to the student union and creating it yourself.

4.5   Judging a university

Age, location, activity and culture are some of the variables in UK universities that you should consider when you apply for a PhD position. But how can you judge how good your university is, compared with others?

There is actually no clear, unambiguous way of doing this. But there are plenty of indicators, published regularly on websites and in broadsheet newspapers. PhD research does not normally involve much tuition, so indicators that rank universities according to staff–student ratios or teaching success may not be very helpful. But one obvious way to assess the capabilities and success of a university is to see how much money it gets for its research. The research councils (described in Chapter 3) publish a list of the recipients of their funding every year. If you want to know which university gets the most money for the kind of work you're interested in, then look up which council funds that topic, and then check the recipient list for that council. Table 4.5 gives the top 25 recipients of MRC (Medical Research Council) funding in 2003/2004. Table 4.6 gives the top 25 recipients of PPARC (Particle Physics and Astronomy Research Council) funding for the same year. You'll notice that the older universities generally receive more funding, but there are a few surprises with some old universities quite weak in certain areas and some newer universities very strong.

Table 4.5 A list of the top 25 largest recipients of MRC grant funding in the 2003/2004 financial year

Rank	Host	£M
1	University of Oxford	19.6
2	University of Cambridge	18.8
3	UCL	16.2
4	Imperial College of Science Technology and Medicine	13.6
5	University of Edinburgh	12.0
6	GKT	9.3
7	University of Manchester	8.1
8	University of Bristol	6.4
9	University of Birmingham	6.2
10	University of Glasgow	4.7
11	Institute of Psychiatry	4.6
12	University of Dundee	4.4
13	London School of Hygiene & Tropical Medicine	4.0
14	University of Leeds	3.9
15	Queen Mary and Westfield College/LHMC/Barts	3.5
16	University of Nottingham	3.3
17	University of Newcastle upon Tyne	3.2
18	University of Leicester	3.0
19	University of Sussex	2.8
20	University of Wales College of Medicine	2.7
21	University of Southampton	2.5
22	University of Liverpool	2.4
23	Institute of Cancer Research	2.3
24	Institute of Child Health (London)	2.3
25	Cardiff University	2.2

Table 4.6 A list of the top 25 largest recipients of PPARC grants for 2004

Rank	Host	£M
1	Queen Mary, University of London	31.5
2	University College London	24.2
3	University of Cambridge	22.4
4	Imperial College London	22.2
5	The University of Manchester	20.2
6	University of Glasgow	19.2
7	University of Oxford	19.2
8	University of Leicester	17.8

9	University of Liverpool	14.7
10	University of Durham	11.9
11	University of Birmingham	10.9
12	Cardiff University	10.2
13	University of Edinburgh	6.4
14	University of Sheffield	5.6
15	Lancaster University	4.7
16	Open University	3.7
17	University of Sussex	3.6
18	University of Southampton	3.2
19	Royal Holloway, University of London	2.8
20	University of Bristol	2.7
21	University of Leeds	2.6
22	Queen's University of Belfast	2.6
23	CCLRC	2.2
24	University of St Andrews	1.9
25	University of Warwick	1.6

Some would argue, quite rightly, that it's not just the money that counts, it's what you do with it that matters. A university does not have to be rich to be good (although it helps). For this reason, every few years there is a national 'research assessment exercise' (RAE) in which the quality and output of staff in all departments of all UK universities are given a score.[13] The score is calculated differently each time, in an attempt to prevent the universities from cheating (which they always try to do by hiring and firing people just beforehand to help optimize their rating). The next RAE is in 2008 and will assess university staff based on:

- research output (usually assessed in terms of the number of scientific publications, such as books, journal and conference papers, and book chapters);
- research environment (measured using factors such as income generated, research degrees awarded, successful dissemination to a broad audience, number of collaborations, and interdisciplinary research);
- esteem (assessed in terms of number of awards, keynote speeches, editorial roles, conference organization and research leadership).

At the time of writing, this assessment had not taken place yet, so we only have the previous RAE results (held in 2001) to examine. The scores are given for each department in a university, with 5 and 5* being the best. You

---

[13] In the 2006 Budget, the government proposed that after 2008, the RAE could be replaced by a metrics-based system.

can find the scores on-line on the 'Higher Education & Research Opportunities in the UK' website: http://www.hero.ac.uk/rae. Table 4.7 lists the 5* departments for four subjects. As you can see, the research ratings are quite varied and sometimes provide a few surprises. It is worth noting that not all of the scores necessarily reflect reality – first, they may be many years out of date, and second, universities have been known to make mistakes or play dirty tricks, which can affect their scores either way.

Table 4.7 Departments in four areas given the top 5 rating in the 2001 research assessment exercise*

5* Geography departments
University of Bristol
University of Durham
Open University
Royal Holloway, University of London
University College London
University of Edinburgh
5* Chemistry departments
University of Bristol
University of Cambridge
University of Durham
Imperial College of Science, Technology and Medicine
University of Oxford
University College London
5* Biological Sciences departments
University of Bristol
University of Cambridge (Biochemistry)
University of Cambridge (Zoology)
Institute of Cancer Research
Imperial College of Science, Technology and Medicine
University of Leicester (Genetics)
University of Manchester
University of Newcastle
University of Sheffield (Animal and Plant Sciences)
University of Sheffield (Molecular and Cellular Biology)
University of Dundee
5* Environmental Science departments
University of East Anglia
University of Reading

The RAE is intended to be the most accurate method, but there are other ways to judge a university, based on its efficiency. The HEFCE 'research performance indicators' measure:

1 the proportion of PhDs awarded per staff costs (how efficient staff are at getting their students to pass their PhDs);
2 the proportion of PhDs awarded per proportion of funding council allocation (how cost-effective are the PhD students – how many funded by the research councils actually pass);
3 the proportion of research grants and contracts obtained per staff (how much cash has each member of staff gained);
4 the proportion of research grants and contracts obtained per proportion of funding council (what proportion of the total cash does the university get).

Again, using 2001 figures, Table 4.8 lists the top five universities. You can download the data yourself from the HEFCE web site (see the resources section).

These metrics are not easily manipulated as they refer to PhD student success rates and financial efficiencies. Nevertheless, when a member of staff moves to a new university, they may take their funding with them, so universities are able to affect these scores (and gain thousands or even millions of pounds) by hiring the right people at the right time. Also note that the metrics used in the RAE measure research output, environment and esteem regardless of where the staff may have spent most of their time.

Table 4.8 The top five bodies in 2001 according to the four research performance indicators

Metric 1	Metric 2
University of East Anglia	Southampton Institute
University of Sussex	Canterbury Christ Church University College
University of Cambridge	University of Wolverhampton
University of Oxford	University College Northampton
Institute of Education	Bournemouth University

Metric 3	Metric 4
Institute of Cancer Research	Institute of Cancer Research
Royal College of Art	London Business School
UoW Centre for Adv Welsh & Celtic Studies	London School of Hygiene & Tropical Medicine
Institute of Education	London School of Economics & Political Science
London School of Hygiene & Tropical Medicine	University College London

So an academic who published 50 papers while at one university could be headhunted by another and the new university would gain all of those publications and money for their RAE rating. Because of this, an old RAE score may be very misleading – the brilliant academics who helped give a department its high rating may have long since departed.

The sad truth is that the more you find out about university lists and ranking methods, the more you realize that none of them are terribly accurate. At best, finding out how rich your department is will tell you how good your PhD facilities are likely to be. Finding out that your department has a top RAE rating will tell you that there are probably some excellent researchers in that department. Discovering that your university does well in the research performance indicators will show you that it is likely to either be very successful in achieving funding, or very efficient at using what it gets.

It is entirely your choice which universities you choose to apply to, for your PhD. Just remember that your priority should be your research. You need to find a place where you will feel comfortable, supported and encouraged to do the best work possible for your doctorate. It really doesn't matter if that university is top or bottom of a list. If it's right for you, then go for it.

5

Finding the right supervisor

The choice of which university is often made because of your supervisor – the person you will work with for many years, who you may cry in front of, curse, and also who will guide and support you through good and bad times. Your supervisor is the most important person in the university. If you can, you need to choose the right person.

5.1　Who are they?

Today there is no excuse for being ignorant about supervisors. It is rapidly becoming policy for all universities to maintain web pages, which describe all members of staff. Most people in academia go much further and maintain extensive personal web pages, describing their teaching, research, students, responsibilities and even their hobbies. This is great news for you. It means that some basic Internet searching will enable you to find out who does what, where. So whether you already know the name of a potential supervisor (perhaps listed in the advertisement for a studentship, or recommended to you by someone at your current or previous university, or even the person who supervised your MSc or undergraduate project) – look them up. If you are limited by where you can live, then go to the websites of the universities in the right area, and use their search options to find the right department, research groups and people.

When you have found some potential names, there are a few basic checks you need to make. First, are they still there? Academics have a tendency to move around, and web pages can take two or three years to catch up with them. Don't set your heart on a supervisor before checking that they haven't emigrated to another continent. A search for up-to-date timetables of lectures by your potential supervisor will tell you where they are. Second, are they allowed to supervise PhD students? In the UK, there are quite a few rules about who can and cannot supervise doctorates. Normally, lecturers, senior lecturers, readers, professors and other full-time staff are allowed to (although a very new lecturer may not be). Contract staff such as research assistants, research fellows, college teachers and research project managers may not be permitted to act as supervisors (because their contracts might run out before the student is finished). Generally, PhD supervisors should have a PhD themselves. An easy way to tell is to find out if they've already got PhD students. (You probably don't want to be their first one, if you can help it.)

Next, you need to find out what they do, in detail. Ideally, you need to get hold of a few recent research papers or a book that they may have written, and read it carefully. Do try to find something recent – academics some-times move to new fields and lose interest in older work. Someone who did something fascinating ten years ago, but has focused on incredibly dull topics since, may not be your best choice. If you cannot find anything on line, don't be afraid of visiting the local university library and digging around, or even ordering a copy. Researching the literature is something you are going to have to do for the next three or four years during your doctorate, so there is no reason why you shouldn't begin now. Do note that academics often have to teach subjects that they have little or no interest in, so don't judge them by their courses, judge them by their research.

5.2   How to contact a supervisor

So you have done your research and found someone whom you think would make a great supervisor. The next step is to get in touch. A good approach is to think about what the supervisor would respond to best.

To help, I'll tell you my own experience as a supervisor. People who would like to begin their PhDs under my supervision contact me frequently. Because I am in a Computer Science department, almost all communication of this type comes via email. And, as long as you're sure that your potential supervisor does actually use email, this can be a very good medium for getting in touch. Email allows you to provide your CV and research interests, and is less likely to be intercepted by a secretary compared to a phone call or letter. You have the opportunity to compose a good piece of writing and not suffer the indignity of nerves or your mind going blank.

But beware. A badly written email enquiry will close doors for you instead of opening them. Here's a typical awful example (Figure 5.1),

```
From: hopeful.student@someyahooadress.com

Subject: doctrel program inquiry

To: someone.obscure, someoneelse.obscure, someother.person,
yetanother.person, … and 58 others.

4 Attachments, 3.6Mb


Dear Sir,


i am very interested in database managment theory .here are my
aplication materiels and i hope you can offer me PHD position.
thank you.


sincerely

hopeful student


attachments: application.doc resume.doc certificate1.doc
certificate2.doc
```

*Figure 5.1 A typical example of a poor email from a prospective student (based on
real examples)*

which will be completely ignored (see if you can spot all the reasons why
this would annoy a potential supervisor).

What's wrong with that? Well, first, the email shows a rather limited
grasp of English spelling and grammar. Remember that most doctorates
involve extensive written work – if even a simple email is too much for a
student, then a whole thesis may be beyond them. Second, (and this is a *big*
mistake) the email was sent to 62 people at once! This indicates that the
student is probably not really serious about their interest in me as a
supervisor, and so why should I be interested in the student? Third, the
student has attached a huge amount of information to the email: the size
of the attachments may have caused my mailer program to crash, and the
attachments themselves are pointless things like scans of degree
certificates. Fourth, the student has expressed an interest in something
that I don't do in my research – clearly he or she has no idea what I do and
has not bothered to find out. Fifth, the student seems to be under the
impression that I will take his application and personally process it.
Applications should be submitted according to the application procedure
of the university, not through a supervisor. Sixth, the email is far too short.
Remember most doctorates involve over three years worth of work with a
supervisor – that's longer than some marriages. A two-sentence enquiry is
madness to initiate such a significant part of your life.

Academics are often very busy people. They may be juggling several
classes of undergraduates and MSc students, a group of PhD researchers,
many collaborators, administrative duties, endless meetings, travel to

conferences, consultancy work and their own research. This level of activity generates a large number of emails every day that require serious attention. If you send an email as bad as the example above, then the chances are that it will simply be deleted without a reply. If you were very lucky, you might get a one-line reply, 'I'm sorry, but I'm not taking any more students this year.'

The only good things about the email was that the student at least had some idea of what he wanted to do, and had attached a CV – not that anyone would read it. If you *really* want to annoy a potential supervisor, then after sending an email like that and receiving no response, try following it up with another email demanding a response. Believe me, you don't find someone to work with by that approach.

Contacting a supervisor is important. It should not be treated in the same way as emailing crazy photos of you at that party last night to all your friends. Your supervisor needs to be able to trust and respect you; he or she needs to know from the beginning that you will be great to work with and that you will gain your doctorate quickly, in an interesting subject. So when you write an email, write it well. Check your spelling and grammar. Address it only to one supervisor and make it personal to them – use their name, mention their research, flatter them by saying how much you enjoyed reading their paper on X or their book on Y. Of course, you may be contacting more than one person – but remember that each potential supervisor has different research interests that will affect you. When you write each email, investigate the research of each person and try to imagine yourself working with each one. If this enquiry works out, then it will really happen with one of them. For goodness sake, don't write pages, and don't attach vast numbers of files. Your initial objective is simply to get a response. If the supervisor is interested, then you can reply with more information.

So what kind of email would I reply to? Something much more like the example in Figure 5.2. Clearly, this student has done her homework. The email is addressed to me alone, the student knows what I do, has read some of my work, is doing a relevant Masters degree, and has attached the kind of information that I need to see: a CV and a short research proposal which will give me an idea of the interests and originality of the student (see Chapter 6 for information about writing your proposal). The email is short, concise, and has no spelling errors. It also contains just enough flattery so that I would feel a little guilty if I did not respond. The request to come and talk also shows that the student is really serious about the enquiry and quite proactive – both good signs. My response would depend on my own circumstances as a supervisor. If I didn't have the time or space for new students, then I would probably reply with a recommendation of someone else. If I thought the CV and research idea were interesting, then I would probably reply with a suggested date and time for a meeting.

```
From: hopeful.student@university.ac.uk
Subject: doctoral programme enquiry
To: peter.bentley
2 Attachments, 45Kb


Dear Prof. Bentley,


I am writing to enquire about PhD positions in your research
group. I am currently completing my MSc on natural computation
and found your book 'Digital Biology' very helpful indeed. I am
very interested in computer models of development and the
origins of the immune system in early life and I have been told
(and can see from your excellent publications) that your
research group specializes in this area.

I attach my CV and a short description of a research project
idea that I hope may interest you. If possible I would like to
come to your lab and discuss this further with you.


sincerely
hopeful student


attachments: cv.doc researchidea.doc
```

Figure 5.2 An example of a good email enquiry to a potential supervisor (based on real examples)

Whether you prefer email, letter, or telephone, your goal should be the same. You need to be known by the supervisor. Your face needs to be familiar and your ideas and enthusiasm memorable. Your supervisor may have to invest a lot of time and effort in you, so you must convince them that it's worth the trouble. The only way you can do that is by building a good rapport with him or her.

Perhaps the most important thing you can learn from this book is: go and talk with potential supervisors. If you rely on an application form alone, then you will never be more than a piece of paper to him or her. To make a good impression, be keen, be enthusiastic and be proactive – send emails, ring him/her on the telephone, and go and talk. Even if you currently live in another country, you should make plans to do this (you need to see the university and accommodation anyway). If you can get a supervisor on your side, getting a PhD place is a hundred times easier.

It is possible that you will not get your first choice of supervisor. Indeed, you may not have any choice at all: the department may have a policy by which they allocate the member of staff whom they consider most appropriate to your research interests. Alternatively, you may be applying for a studentship, which is being offered under one specific supervisor. Whatever the situation, the same point applies: you need to go and meet this person as soon as possible. If you two don't get along, then it doesn't matter how great everything else might be, you'll be in trouble. If you do get along, then even serious problems (such as funding or research directions) become very much easier to handle, throughout your doctorate.

5.3   Do you get on well with him or her?

When you go and talk with the potential supervisor, he or she will be judging you, maybe even giving you a mini interview (see interviews later). But it is just as important that you interview him or her. You need to make sure you both get along. Is there mutual respect? Can you bear to be in his or her company? Do you both believe similar things are exciting and important in research? If the answer is no to any of these, then there will be severe problems later.

It is always worth talking with the supervisor's other students. You will then obtain the best description of what it's like to be a student of this supervisor. Of course they might have a different personality and abilities to you, so their relationship might be different. But you will get a broad picture, for example, maybe the supervisor is away at meetings so much that the students never see him. Maybe the students feel trapped by the level of control imposed on them. Maybe the supervisor has a horrible temper and flies into a rage every other day. It's nice to find these things out *before* you start.

Personality conflicts with supervisors are a surprisingly common source of problems for PhD students. Remember, this is someone you'll have to work with for the next three or four years. You may think that you're great with all kinds of people and there'll be no problem. But three or four years is more than enough time for you both to see the worst of each other; you'll both have lots of really bad days, misunderstandings and arguments. People are all different, and you need to judge for yourself whether you can get along with your supervisor or not. All I can do here is give a few clues to watch for.

Here's one sad fact: intelligent people are not always nice people. They're certainly not always easy to get along with. You'll find that many academics have quite impressive egos – their belief in themselves and the significance of their work is often excessive. Yes, he may be a professor who has authored a few books, but no, that doesn't make him the world's authority on life, the universe and everything. An ambitious academic may seem like a cross between a visionary and a bully. He may know exactly where he wants the research to go, and he may be quite ruthless in his goal to ensure it happens – so watch out! A more experienced academic may seem like a cross between an oracle and a politician – she seems to know everything and everyone, but somehow is a little out of touch with the real world and always answers a question in her own terms. You may be a little uncertain where you stand with such people.

There are some warning signs to look out for between you and your supervisor. Certain personality traits can be dominant, or provocative, such as being very imaginative, strong-minded, argumentative and self-confident. If you share the same trait with your supervisor, for example, if you are both very imaginative or both very strong-willed, there is likely to be some conflict in your future relationship. Other personality traits are more conciliatory, such as being open-minded, flexible, assiduous and considerate. If you share the same conciliatory trait as your supervisor, for example, if you are both very easy going and flexible, then you may not have enough drive pushing you to make good progress and your work may stagnate. Academics are usually fairly provocative (since we like to believe we know what we're talking about), and so a common supervisor–student relationship will be formed with the supervisor taking the dominant provocative role and the student taking the conciliatory role to begin with. Then as the student becomes more experienced and gains confidence, the roles often switch, with the student becoming the provocateur and the supervisor letting go of the reins and becoming a conciliator (see Table 5.1).

Whatever the dynamics of your personalities, it is vital that you both create and maintain mutual respect for and trust of each other. You must be able to trust that your supervisor will always be there for you, guiding you when you need help, even if you may not always like what is said to you. Your supervisor needs to be able to trust that you can do what you say you can do, and that you will admit you need help whenever the occasion arises.

Some supervisors (and I'm one of them) like to believe that maintaining a close, friendly team helps everyone work well and be happy. Others like to maintain a distance, enabling them to keep the distinction between supervisor and student clear. This is the choice of the supervisor, with the busier, older supervisors generally preferring not to make close friendships, simply because it's easier. I prefer, if I can, to become friends with my

Table 5.1 Different personality traits in supervisor and student produce different results in your progress

Supervisor	Student	Result
Provocative	Provocative	Conflict
Conciliatory	Conciliatory	Stagnation
Provocative	Conciliatory	Supervisor-led progress
Conciliatory	Provocative	Student-led progress

students. Indeed, some of my best friends are my old PhD students. I've participated in their weddings, we socialize together and some of them come back years later and work with me as colleagues. But friendships in a supervisor–student relationship can be complex. There are times when a supervisor has to say things that a friend could not, and equally, there are times when a student must respect the guidance of their supervisor on their work more than they might respect the guidance of a friend. In the end, while you're doing your PhD, the relationship between you and your supervisor is unequal, however close your friendship might become.

5.4 How much time will he or she have for you?

Supervisors tend to work quite differently, depending on their personalities and time constraints. Some are very 'hands on' – they will want to work with you much of the time, suggesting new ideas, helping you perform your research. Some are the opposite – they may not see you for a month or two at a time and they may expect you to get on with things without much help. Part of this may be dictated by the research culture at the relevant university or department. Some chemistry labs, for example, require a group of researchers to work together constantly and may require regular and close direction from a supervisor. In contrast, a doctoral student in mathematics may not even see his supervisor for a year, while he develops his own ideas.

Generally, all doctoral students require guidance through the course of their work. You are usually expected to pass through certain progress assessments, which may go under the names of 'first-year viva' and 'transfer viva'. You may be expected to take courses or study for preliminary qualifications first. You could be expected to write papers in journals and present your work at conferences. You'll need to show that you can be original and have skills such as analysis and critical review. Your thesis will have to be rigorous and follow the correct format for your subject and your university. It doesn't matter how clever you are, you'll need guidance at some point with some of these issues.

Increasingly, universities are introducing regulations to ensure that students receive the contact time they are entitled to with their supervisors. University College London, for example, has introduced a compulsory 'logbook' scheme in which PhD students must record details of supervisory meetings each quarter. Figure 5.3 shows an example page from the logbook to give you an idea of what students and supervisors might need to discuss. But whether your university has such strict controls or not, the amount of time you will get with your supervisor is something you need to check on.

To be completed by the student before supervisory session
What progress have you achieved during the last 3 months?

I performed a literature review on T-cell regulation and helped out in the lab.

Did you encounter any difficulties?
Yes X No

If yes, explain briefly

My background in Organic Chemistry did not prepare me for the Immunobiology terminology, which I'm finding hard to follow

Have there been any changes to your skills development plans?
Yes No X N/A

Comments

Are there other skills you may want to develop?
Yes X No N/A

I'd like to know about Ethics in Biology

Any agreed changes to direction of research?
Yes X No N/A

We agreed that a focus on more practical work and on lower level processes might exploit my chemistry experience more

Particular academic needs identified
Yes X No N/A

I feel that I would benefit from more regular meetings with Prof White and other members of his group.

Agreed research plan and activities

Focus on TLRs and begin work in the lab optimising samples 1 to 16

Time frame

Finish above in next 3 months

Figure 5.3 A (fictional) page from the University College London student's logbook

Every student is different, and requires a different level of support. You can get an idea of how much time you will need by trying the following exercise. Imagine you need to solve a difficult and perhaps unusual problem. Let us say you must figure out a way to herd five cats into a pen (without using food or catnip). You've got one week to find the best possible solution to this dilemma. What are you going to do? Before reading on, try writing down the steps you would take to solve the problem. Be completely honest with yourself.

So, what did you write down? I suspect it was one of these:

1 I don't know what I'd do.
2 I'd try to talk to other people about the problem.
3 I'd get some cats and try out different ideas herding them.
4 I'd go and think about the problem for a while, perhaps finding something to read on the subject, and figure out the best solution.

If your answer was (1) or (2), then you may be the kind of person who prefers a more hands-on supervisor, who would be able to suggest how to start tackling the problem and where to look for more information about it. If your answer was (3) or (4), then you may be a more independent student who prefers to be left alone to solve problems by yourself. Another way you can tell what kind of person you are is by assessing the way you behaved during an undergraduate or MSc project. Did you feel that you needed help fairly often or were you happy to work on your own?

Even if you do consider yourself to be very independent, a good supervisor will still be able to assist you. In the problem above, your supervisor would at the very least help you define a timetable to work to, ensuring that you spend the right amount of time on each part of the solution. The supervisor would also keep challenging a good student to help them improve: so your solution works for the cats in your garden, but what about five lions?

You know yourself best. When you go and talk with a potential supervisor and her students, ask how hands-on she is. If you're the independent type, make sure she's 'hands-off' (or is often very busy). If you prefer to work with closer guidance, then make sure she's the 'hands-on' type (or that she will always have time available for you). The supervisor will be trying to judge exactly the same thing with you. The last thing she wants is for you to become depressed after a year because you feel you never get any help, or because you're never given any space to work on your own. If things aren't satisfactory, it is possible to change supervisors after you've begun your doctorate, but (depending on the department and the circumstances) that can sometimes be a drawn-out and complicated process. It is much easier if you can begin with someone who is right for you. You need to make sure you get the kind of supervision you need.

5.5 Is he or she experienced at supervising?

Before you have surgery it's usually wise to ask your surgeon a few questions. How many times have you performed this operation? How long have you been a surgeon? What percentage of the time does something go wrong? The same thing applies before you begin a PhD with a supervisor. You need to know how many times the supervisor has successfully supervised a PhD to completion. You need to know how long they have been supervising students. And you need to know how well the supervisor is able to supervise.

Remember that supervisors have to learn how to supervise. Even the best of us have to start somewhere, and if you are his first PhD student, you may be in for a rough ride. Generally, the more students the supervisor has taken to completion, the better that supervisor will be with you. A young, enthusiastic supervisor with eight PhD students may sound great, but if he has never successfully managed to get one their PhD, then eight PhD students plus you might be just enough to give him a nervous breakdown and leave you wondering what to do next.

Beware of the inexperienced supervisor when you go and talk to him. He may be a lovely person and very complimentary and enthusiastic. He may tell you on the spot that you'll be offered a place to work with him and you'll get funding. But promises made by an inexperienced academic can tragically turn out to be false. The funding is much more likely to fall through and the position may never appear. The supervisor may be so excited at the prospect of getting you that he promises more than he can deliver. Don't believe anything until you have it in writing from an official university administrator.

Supervisors need to learn as much as you do, during your PhD. They need to understand that you need different guidance as your skills (and emotional states) change. They need to understand that giving detailed technical support is often less important than helping you to learn your own technical skills. They need to learn that they are there to provide a service: to help you do what you want to do, and not treat you like their personal slave. They need to discover that being aware of your moods (which may vary from wonderful excitement to severe depression) is just as important as being aware of your abilities. They also need to know when to be nice and when to be firm.

A good supervisor will be able to guide you to an exciting niche – something new that has not been done before. She will help you find a subject that you are interested in and that she and her group are interested in. Hopefully, the topic will be significant, useful and will help you to get where you want to go in life. A good supervisor might help bring you academic reputation, public fame, or the start of your own business.

All of these skills come with experience and there are few courses to teach the details. Supervisors just make it up as they go along, which means that if you are one of their first students, you'll experience many of their mistakes as they learn. Of course, some people just make great supervisors, and others never get the hang of it. A good supervisor will make your doctorate go like a dream (as long as you listen to her advice). A bad supervisor can result in you wasting years of your time and money, and probably make you terribly depressed while it's happening. For your own sake, it's really worth the effort of trying to find a good one.

So how can you tell? Luckily, experience is measurable. Ask the right questions and find out how many students have got their PhDs under this supervisor. If the answer is zero, then be careful. You will need to make sure you get an experienced second supervisor as a back-up. Ask how long he has been supervising students. You're looking for lots of time and lots of successful students. If he's been a supervisor for ten years, but has only got two through, that's not great. If he's been a supervisor for ten years and have got five or six through, that's good. Ask if any of his students have given up or moved to other labs. Good supervisors have students prepared to follow them even if they move to a different university. A bad supervisor will not be able to keep students longer than a couple of years before they give up. Again, if you can, talk to his current students – they'll give you the best idea of what to expect.

5.6   What stage of career is he or she at?

Your main supervisor will almost always be an academic member of staff. He or she will have their job for a reason, and (in their mind) that reason is not primarily to help you. Sometimes, because of their own ambitions, academics may move universities or change jobs. As his or her student, you need to be aware of your supervisor's motivations, for they might affect you.

As you may have noticed during your previous degree, academic staff can be a mixed bunch of (sometimes strange) personalities, ranging from the highly ambitious communicators to the socially inept introverts. You might find yourself with a 'professor wannabe' – someone whose entire goal in life is to work his way up through the ranks, often jumping from university to university, until he reaches his goals. This kind of ambition means that such staff will often have large groups of PhD students (sometimes too large) and may spend a little too much time thinking about their career instead of helping you with yours. Even when he becomes a professor, he may still keep pushing: positions like Head of Department, Dean of the School and upwards, may beckon him. His career will always come first, so when he moves on, you may be forced to follow him to a new university or stay and find a new supervisor. However, you can also benefit from an ambitious supervisor, because he may well be going places and becoming famous in the field, and helping to shine the spotlight on your work.

Alternatively, your supervisor might resemble a 'tired teacher' – someone who stays at the same university for most of his life, rarely achieves promotion, spends most of his time lecturing and rarely takes on PhD students. Such staff may have little interest in research and little motivation to help you. But you might have a lot of freedom to do what you want without interference.

Or your supervisor might be ex-industry. These are people who may have spent years in industry before giving it up (and giving up a good salary) in search of a more interesting life. Such staff often have a wealth of practical knowledge, are quite excited by research and its opportunities, but may take a while to understand how the university research system operates. If you want practical real-world knowledge, such a supervisor could be great.

Another supervisor type is the salesmen or businessmen – they are so interested in talking about or exploiting the results of the research, either through the media or via industry, that they may exploit you. It is really not great to find yourself acting like an unpaid employee of a new company instead of a PhD student.

Some supervisors are 'fashion-hoppers' – they never stay with one research topic more than a year or two before hopping to the next fashionable area, as a trick to secure funding or increase their fame. You may have a lot of fun while you're in fashion, but if your work doesn't fit with his picture any more, you may be sidelined.

And some supervisors are 'born researchers' – not always very interested in teaching or careers, but totally dedicated to their research and their vision. These researchers are easy to spot because of their large publication record; but their ability to supervise you is completely unrelated to their work. Some wonderful researchers are appalling supervisors; some are superb. Your supervisor is likely to have one or more of these common traits. (Figure 5.4 provides a few other amusing examples relating to principal investigators, drawn by immunobiologist Prof Alex Dent.)

It's worthwhile looking at their backgrounds (again the Internet is invaluable for this) and working out what his or her motivations are, and whether they severely conflict with yours. If you have no interest in starting a company, for example, and your supervisor is mainly interested in developing something which leads to a product for a company, then you may not be comfortable. Or if you have ethical problems about the military, you may not be happy with a supervisor who regularly obtains funding from the Ministry of Defence.

Because academics may begin life in academia at any age after their mid-twenties, you can't judge their career progression from their age. Sometimes academics can be young and very experienced, or older and very inexperienced. However, a new academic is more likely to be ambitious and keen to build a group. A more experienced academic may be less enthusiastic about taking on new students, but may be more reliable and better able to help you.

Figure 5.4 Principal investigators are academics in charge of a funded research project – which might be your PhD. Which one is your supervisor?

(Alex Dent, for The NIH Catalyst, 1995, reproduced with permission)

5.7   Second supervisors

In most universities, you will be able to choose a second supervisor some time after you have begun your doctorate. If you are doing an engineering doctorate, you may have an academic supervisor and an industrial supervisor to guide you, in which case, both will be decided at the start. It is important that you do find yourself a second supervisor at some stage (and some students even have three). However good your primary supervisor is, it is important to have a second opinion. You may only see the second supervisor a few times during the course of your work, but if something goes wrong, the second supervisor will be able to guide you and tell you your options. Sometimes a student may even choose to swap their first and second supervisors. This is a quick and easy way to change your supervisor without causing too many problems.

If your project is interdisciplinary or a joint academic/industrial project, then twin supervisors are essential. You need one supervisor who is a specialist in each area. So if your work is mathematical modelling of the immune system, you need a mathematician and an immunobiologist. Alternatively, if you discover that your supervisor is not helping you in the way you feel you need, a carefully chosen second supervisor can resolve your problems. Some inexperienced supervisors believe that they should be the one and only person to help you. They are wrong. This is your doctorate and your life, and having a second opinion (whether you agree with it or not) is always beneficial.

6
Finding the right research project

Once you've picked your ideal university and supervisor, you need to figure out what your research project will be. Except for studentships, where the project is already defined, all PhDs require the student to outline their proposed research project before they begin. Your research proposal is the most important way of informing the department and your potential supervisor about your research interests and ambitions. As we saw in Chapter 5, it is common for students to initiate communication with potential supervisors by sending their proposals. Make a bad job of this document, and you will eliminate your chances of working with the supervisor or even joining a university. Do a good job, and you may get a huge amount of support and assistance. But how do you figure out what to write? What makes a good PhD project?

6.1   How to be different

Thinking of a project worthy of a PhD is quite easy if you are an academic with several years of experience of supervising PhDs. But it's not easy at all if you're an undergraduate or MSc student. PhD projects are orders of magnitude harder than anything taught or any project performed in these degrees. Without several years of research experience and large amounts of knowledge of what has been done already, it's very hard to suggest a project that is hard enough to be significant, but not so hard that you'll never be able to do it.

   PhD research is sometimes said to be about 'making a contribution to world knowledge' (although there are many other definitions, depending on the type of doctorate you are doing, as we saw in Chapter 2). That means that the research project must be ambitious and imaginative enough to be different and useful, but not so ambitious that you'll never make any progress. It's often a good idea to continue something you know – such as extending or expanding on your MSc project.

Your project will also influence your future. A highly theoretical project will make it much harder for you to find a job in industry. A very applied project in collaboration with a company may make it harder for you to continue your research in academia. Either way, you will become known for your PhD work, and you'll find that the next job you take (whether in industry or academia) will be in a similar area. PhDs often cause people to specialize so much that it can take them several years to 'escape' from their field, should they want to. So it is a good idea to find a PhD project that you find fascinating and are prepared to pursue beyond the end of your PhD.

A good trick is to try and find a very new area that is just beginning to take off. There may be several very recent scientific publications on the topic and perhaps a new research group on the topic. You're looking for something that is not too new, and not too well established. If it's too new, the whole idea may turn out to be terminally flawed – you won't want to work for three years and then find that the whole thing was a mistake. In contrast, if it has been around for a long time, you'll find that you will be competing with hundreds or even thousands of other researchers – you may find it impossible to be noticed in the crowd. In the worst case, the area may have died out – there may be thousands of publications, but nothing recent. If you try to suggest a project in an area like that, you're in danger of looking out of date.

Performing research is rather like surfing a wave. It's very important to pick a good wave that will carry you far. If there's no one else there, that may be a sign that it's not a great choice. If it's too crowded, you'll find it really hard to make progress without others getting in your way. Choose well, and you'll be able to make your way to the crest and keep yourself at the front all the way. If you can surf to the front of the research field and stay there, then by the time you achieve your doctorate you may be quite famous and be known as someone at the top of the field. That will be very useful for you and your future.

There are other slightly cynical tricks that some people use. It's well known that a healthy (positive) interest from the media can boost the career of an academic. The media mainly respond to visually interesting work or results that can be explained simply, but that have wide-reaching significance. This is why work such as novel robots are often reported in the press – they are visually appealing. It's also why DNA computers that might cure cancer make the news – the idea can be explained in one sentence and would have a significant impact on all of us. But a word of warning: the media also respond to academics who claim to have evidence that contradicts well-established scientific fact. The 'controversial approach' is not advisable unless you have irrefutable evidence that you're right (and it's much more likely that you're wrong and everyone else is right). Shouting crazy ideas to the willing media will result in your colleagues accusing you of being a 'media whore', and ruining all hope of a respectable research career.

A less public approach is to try to think of a research project that may lead to a commercially lucrative product. Whether a new drug, a new material or a new type of computer, if your work is likely to have a high financial impact then you may become very popular, and well known. Again, that's great for your future – just be careful that your ideas are not stolen by those who want to make profits.

You'll find that academics will respond quite differently to different types of ideas. Some prefer students to be ambitious and try to aim high. Few ambitious students ever achieve everything they'd like to, but their motivation to achieve a grand goal can often help them to overcome the difficulties they'll face along the way. Grand goals can enable students to use their doctorate to make a difference in the world and do something significant that will have a real impact on others.

Some academics prefer a quieter life and do not encourage lofty and unachievable ambitions. They prefer to focus on the details of a problem and ensure every part is analysed and understood. If you approach someone like this to be your supervisor, you'll find that your proposal will need to be technically detailed and may have a very focused and narrow scope. Clearly you should be the kind of person who finds this form of highly-focused research fascinating if you find yourself with this kind of project.

Whatever your ambitions are, choosing exactly the right project is difficult. It is so difficult that universities fully expect students to alter the details of their proposals during the course of their work. So don't think that the idea you have now will actually form the main part of your thesis. It may, but the chances are that after a year or two your ideas will develop and grow, taking you to a slightly different place.

6.2 Writing a proposal

Writing is one of those skills that you develop through ~
your doctorate, you will have to learn how to write '
for your research area. In science, this means a v
structure. No one expects you to know how to do
proposal, but the closer you come to the re(
impressive your application will be. Your writing
other aspects about you. It will indicate the compe
language and grammar. It will give a suggestion of

your intelligence. It will also indicate your motivation for doing a PhD. All of these aspects will be used to judge your competence, and likely ability to complete a doctorate.

Nevertheless, the most important thing to get right in your proposal is not the style, but the content. A PhD research proposal needs to explain several important things such as:

1 why you want to do a PhD;
2 where your idea comes from and its similarity to existing work;
3 your research goals;
4 how you intend to achieve your goals.

To give an idea of the kinds of applications we often receive from students, take a look at Figures 6.1 and 6.2. The exceptionally short example in Figure 6.1 shows a very poor proposal. Why is it so bad? First, it provides unnecessary details about the student's academic background (which will be included in other areas of the application form). Second, it shows zero imagination (it doesn't actually suggest a research project at all) and seems to indicate that the applicant has not really thought about what they would like to do. Third, the reason given for wishing to do a PhD seems to indicate a misunderstanding of the nature of a doctorate. The way it is written suggests that the student is used to being taught courses but shows no recognition that in a PhD they must perform research on their own and not rely on formal tuition. Such students often achieve great exam results but do poorly in projects because they do not enjoy working without constant guidance. Finally, the proposal is too short, not very well written with repeated words, punctuation errors, mistakes such as 'PHd' instead of 'PhD' and shows a childish naivety which does not help convince the reader that the applicant is intelligent or mature enough to begin a doctorate. Based on this proposal alone, this student would be unlikely to find a supervisor and thus would be unlikely to be accepted in a university.

Contrast this with the great example given in Figure 6.2.[14] This is unusually well written – in fact, it is highly unusual to see a proposal

I spent the last three years studying my BSc course on Engineering + Technology which; I found very interesting especially the subject on different materials used in glass houses which I thought was very interesting. Before that I did many subjects at sixth form college including; electronics and physics which were good. I haven't got any ideas yet but I would like to do PHd on an interesting subject and will learn new areas if you think I need to. I think I would enjoy doing a PHd because; I liked being taught about interesting subjects.

Figure 6.1 An example of a very poor research proposal written by a PhD applicant (based on real examples).

Thanks to Saoirse for his permission to reproduce his actual proposal in this book. certainly got my attention when he sent me such a good piece of work when ng me if I would supervise him for his PhD.

Evolving Particle Interactions that Lead to Particle Synchronization for Ubiquitous Computing Environments

Saoirse Amarteifio

Abstract—Hypothesis: Evolutionary algorithms in conjunction with agent-based swarm modeling can be used to derive particle behaviours that promote synergy or *culture* for ubiquitous computing environments enabling adaptive behaviour.

I. INTRODUCTION

Ever-shrinking mobile devices, wireless networks, semantic protocols, component architectures, autonomous agents and people comprise a vast and complex *infosphere*[1] that begins to rival biological systems in complexity but not in self-organizing, adaptive behaviour. This artificial network has stagnated at a point overcome by biological systems millions of years ago. The question one might ask is how did the ant evolve into a homeostatic ant colony? Or similarly, how did multicellular systems emerge at increasingly complex scales? This phenomenon is termed *synergenesis* and as used here, has been especially formulated for adding *culture* to ubiquitous computing environments in an elegant, biologically inspired manner.

A. What is Culture?

In the language of Synergetics and complexity, culture constitutes the *order parameters* while individual behaviours constitute the control parameters [2]. While order parameters emerge from the dynamics of control parameters, they in turn regulate the control parameters. This gives way to interesting emergent behaviour as seen in societies, economies, physical systems and biological systems [2], [3]. This seems to create a chicken-and-egg conundrum where it becomes unclear whether culture determines the behaviours of individuals or individual behaviours determine culture. The *origin* of such culture is referred to here as synergenesis.

Consider an example where ants, deposit pheromone and move to regions of high pheromone concentration [4]. Initially ants seem to move randomly. After a time, assuming appropriate parameter settings for pheromone evaporation and diffusion rates, regions of the space become favoured as pheromone depositing ants reinforce emerging trails through autocatalysis. What is interesting to note with respect to our previous discussion on culture, is that ants both create and react to the same environment as their space becomes ordered. The ants create the culture that they are subsequently controlled by!

II. BACKGROUND

A. Evolutionary Algorithms

Evolutionary algorithms and their biological basis have evolved from the very abstract genetic algorithm [5] and genetic programming [6] methods, based loosely on Darwin's survival of the fittest paradigm and Mendelian genetics, to increasingly rich models based on developmental biology or design by morphogenesis [7], [8], [9], [10], [11], [12]. Generative encodings and cellular automata [13], [14], [15], neural network architectures [16], *growth* of designs [7] or swarms [17] respect and involve the natural regularities of the environment in which they are evolving a structure. As such it is necessary that the solution is 'played out' to determine fitness.

There have been a huge number of diverse applications of evolutionary algorithms over the last couple of decades. The general methodology is that a problem is encoded in a binary or real valued string or genome. The genome is mapped to the program or model and evaluated in order to assign fitness to the genotype. The fittest solutions are given greater propagation rights, similar to any species within the Darwinian survival of the fittest paradigm. In this way it is expected that solutions become increasingly fit.

B. Swarm Intelligence

The term *swarm intelligence* has been used in more than one context [18], [19]. As used here, it is derived from [19] but concentrates on fundamental information processing principles rather than algorithms. Following extensive studies on mass action in natural ant colonies such as [20], [21], many algorithms have been developed based on ant colony optimization for optimization and real world problems[22], [23], [24], [19], [25]. Swarms are an ideal form of artificial intelligence for real world systems due to their continuous, spatially extended, loosely connected topologies. Of course ant colonies are just one type of spatially extended system in nature. The immune system is another well-studied example and like the ant colony [4], it is also seen as a cognitive system [26]. Biological systems operate over extended spatial regions through local activation long range inhibition (LALI) mechanisms [27]. [28] discuss the computational potential of societies of active cognitive transducers.

Figure 6.2 An example of a very good (real) scientific research proposal written by a PhD applicant

2

C. Ubiquity

Ubiquitous computing is characterized be *seamless* integration of *networked* information systems as envisioned by Mark Weiser [29]. This is becoming possible due to the shrinking of smart devices and growth of wireless networking technologies to enable *embedded networks* [30]. These types of systems are *embodied* in their environment and may include sensor networks and personal or business ad hoc device networks. Seamless embodiment requires context sensitivity for appropriate behaviour based on local events and without continuous user intervention. Context is simply information that can be used to characterize a situation and thus affect the appropriate reaction [31]. [32] propose that a considerable portion of what we call 'intelligence' in Artificial Intelligence or 'good design' in Human-Computer Interaction actually amounts to being sensitive to context.

Spatially extended embedded network systems have specific system assembly and maintenance requirements. They require *real-time local decision making* appropriate to macroscopic goals, ad hoc resource discovery and composition, ad hoc complex interactions, *continuous monitoring* in long-lived systems and recovery [30]. Existing embedded network systems are highly *data and event driven* [33].

Biological systems, which are also event and data driven, achieve system assembly and maintenance respectively through embryological development and immune systems preservation of self. Each of these 'multicellular systems' are based on the same adaptive design principles and mechanisms [26], which are undoubtedly relevant to ubiquitous computing infrastructures.

III. METHODOLOGY

A. First High-Level Deliverable

The first element of the proposed model uses grammar-based evolution and functional induction. The function should be an appropriate model of local information and grammars define legal interpretations of local information. Such work has already been carried out by the author [34]. This can be described as an *emergent computation reverse-engineering framework* [35]. This model will be developed further and applied to biological models to develop adaptive multicellular system regulation methods through evolution. The primary difficulty is the fitness evaluation function or quantification of macroscopic objectives [36], [15].

B. Second High-Level Deliverable

The developed framework will be applied to control problems in sensor networks, ad hoc device assembly and certain cases of component composition. Each node in these systems will be modeled as a particle with given behaviours. Regulation of these behaviours through evolved functions allows the macroscopic system to become synchronized in the cultural sense described above. An embodied synchronized systems may be highly adaptive and seem anticipatory [37]. As in biological systems, the evolved part of the system is entirely context sensitive. Grammars are used to formally model legal interpretations of local data and events considering the fact that these systems are data and event driven [33]. Methods to model relevant information in grammars in addition to methods for determining fitness functions are an important research objective.

REFERENCES

[1] L. Floidi, *Philosophy and computing: an introduction.* Routledge, 1999.
[2] H. Haken, "Synergetics: An overview," in *Emergence in Complex, Cognitive, Social, and Biological Systems,* G. Minati and E. Pessa, Eds. Kluwer Academic/Plenum Publishers, 2002.
[3] A. S. Mikhailov and V. Calenbuhr, *From Cells to Societies: Models of Complex Coherent Action.* Spring Verlag, 2002.
[4] D. Chialvo and M. Millonas, "How swarms build cognitive maps," in *The biology and technology of intelligent autonomous agents,* L. Steels, Ed. NATO ASI Series, 1995, pp. 439–450.
[5] J. H. Holland, *Adaptation in Natural and Artifical Systems.* MIT Press Edition, 1992, 1992.
[6] J. Koza, *Genetic Programming: On the Programming of Computers by Means of Natural Selection.* MIT Press, 1992.
[7] P. Bentley and S. Kumar, "Three ways to grow designs: A comparison of embryogenics for an evolutionary design problem," in *Proceedings of the Genetic and Evolutionary Computation Conference,* W. Banzhaf, J. Daida, A. E. Eiben, M. H. Garzon, V. Honavar, M. Jakiela, and R. E. Smith, Eds., vol. 1. Orlando, Florida, USA: Morgan Kaufmann, 13-17 July 1999, pp. 35–43.
[8] J. C. Bongard and R. Pfeifer, "Repeated structure and dissociation of genotypic and phenotypic complexity in artificial ontogeny," in *Proceedings of The Genetic and Evolutionary Computation Conference, GECCO-2001,* ser. Lecture Notes in Artificial Intelligence, L. Spector, Ed., vol. 2801. Morgan Kaufmann publishers, 14-17 Sept. 2001, pp. 256–265.
[9] W. Banzhaf, T. Christaller, P. Dittrich, J. T. Kim, and J. Ziegler, Eds., *Evolving Developmental Programs for Adaptation, Morphogenesis, and Self-Repair,* ser. Lecture Notes in Artificial Intelligence, vol. 2801. Dortmund, Germany: Springer, 14-17 Sept. 2003.
[10] J. Lehre and P. Haddow, "Developmental mappings and phenotypic complexity," in *Proceedings of CEC,* 2003, pp. 62–68.
[11] P. J. Bentley, "Fractal proteins," *Genetic Programming and Evolvable Machines,* vol. 5, no. 1, pp. 71–101, 2004.
[12] J. Federici and D. Roggen, "Multi-cellular development: is there scalability and robustness to gain?" in *Proceedings of Parallel Problem Solving from Nature,* no. 8, San Francisco, 2004, pp. 391–400.
[13] J. Crutchfield, M. Mitchell, and R. Das, "Evolving cellular automata with genetic algorithms: A review of recent work," in *In Proceedings of the First International Conference on Evolutionary Computation and its Applications,* 1996.
[14] W. Hordjik, "Dynamics, emergent computation, and evolution in cellular automata," Ph.D. dissertation, Univesity New Mexico, 1999.
[15] J. Crutchfield, M. Mitchell, and R. Das, "Evolutionary design of collective computation in cellular automata," in *Evolutionary Dynamics,* J. Crutchfield and P. Schuster, Eds. Oxford University Press, 2003.
[16] H. Kitano, "Designing neural networks using genetic algorithms with graph generation system," *Complex Systems,* vol. 4, 1990.
[17] M. Oneill and T. Brabazon, "Grammatical swarm," in *GECCO,* 2004.
[18] J. Kennedy and R. Eberhart, *Swarm Intelligence.* Morgan Kaufmann, 2001.
[19] E. Bonabeau, G. Theraulaz, and M. Dorigo, *Swarm Intelligence.* Oxford Press, 1999.
[20] E. O. Wilson, *The Social Insects.* Harvard University Press, 1971.
[21] B. Hölldobler and E. O. Wilson, *The Ants.* Sprinter-Verlag, 1990.
[22] A. Colorini, M. Dorigo, and V. Maniezzo, "Distributed optimisation by ant colonies," in *European Conference on Artifical Life,* F. Varela and P. Bourgine, Eds. MIT-Press, 1991, pp. 134–142.
[23] M. Dorigo, V. Maniezzo, and A. Colorini, "Ant system: Optimization by a colony of cooperating agents," *IEEE Transactions,* pp. 29–41, 1996.
[24] C. A. Silva, T. A. Runkler, J. M. da Costa Sousa, and R. Palm, "Ant colonies as logistic processes optimizers." in *Ant Algorithms,* 2002, pp. 76–87.
[25] E. Bonabeau, F. Henaux, S. Guérin, D. Snyers, P. Kuntz, and G. Theraulaz, "Routing in telecommunications networks with "smart" ant-like agents," Santa Fe Institute, Tech. Rep. 98-01-003, Jan. 1998.
[26] I. R. Cohen, *Tending Adam's Garden: Evolving The Cognitive Immune Self.* Academic Press, 2000.

Figure 6.2 (continued) An example of a very good (real) scientific research proposal written by a PhD applicant

3

[27] E. Bonabeau, "From classical models of morphogenesis to agent-based models of pattern formation," *Artificial Life 3*, pp. 191–209, 1997.

[28] J. Wiedermann and J. Van Leeuwen, "Emergent computational potential of evolving artificial living systems," *AI Communications 15*, pp. 205–215, 1999.

[29] M. Weiser, "The computer for the 21st century," *Scientific America*, 1991.

[30] C. S. Committee on Networked Systems of Embedded Computers and T. Board, *A Research Agenda for Networked Systems of Embedded Computers*. National Academic Press, Washington, 2001.

[31] D. S. Anind K. Dey and G. D. Abowd, "A conceptual framework and a toolkit for supporting the rapid prototyping of context-aware applications," *Human-Computer Interaction, special issue on context-aware computing*, vol. 16, no. 2-4, 2001.

[32] H. Lieberman and T. Selker, "Out of context: Computer systems that adapt to and learn from context," *IBM Rsearch Journal*, vol. 39, no. 3-4, 2000.

[33] H. Abelson, D. Allen, D. Coore, C. Hanson, G. Homsy, T. F. Knight, R. Nagpal, E. Rauch, G. J. Sussman, and R. Weiss, "Amorphous computing," *Communications of the ACM*, vol. 43, no. 5, pp. 74–82, 2000.

[34] Saoirse Amarteifio and Michael O'Neill, "An evolutionary approach to complex system regulation using grammatical evolution," in *Artificial Life IX (Proceedings of the Ninth International Conference on the Simulation and Synthesis of Living Systems)*, 2004.

[35] A. Kubrik, "Towards a formalisation of emergence," *Artifical Life*, vol. 9, pp. 41-65, 2003.

[36] R. Nagpal, "Programmable self-assembly using biologically-inspired multiagent control," *First International Joint Conference on Autonomous Agents and Multi-Agent Systems*, pp. 418–425, 2002.

[37] R. Rosen, *Anticipatory Systems: Philosophical, Mathematical and Methodological Foundations*. Pergamon Press, 1985.

Figure 6.2 (continued) An example of a very good (real) scientific research proposal written by a PhD applicant

written in a scientific format used for scientific publications. You don't need to understand the research in this proposal to see what's good about it. It should be clear that the applicant knows the field of research and knows which existing work relates to his ideas. (He demonstrates this by referring to a scientific paper authored by him, which is also very impressive.) He has clearly stated his interests and even provided a clear research hypothesis – not something we expect to see until after a year or more of PhD research. He has also described what he would like to do for his research and how he proposes to achieve it. The one thing missing is a description of why he wants to do a PhD – but in this case, the quality of writing, evidence of previous successful research, and mature scientific style give a very strong indication that this candidate is keen to perform research and understands what it entails.

No university expects a proposal formatted in quite such a rigorous scientific style, so don't copy this example. The most important thing is that you need to get your ideas across clearly, communicate your motivation and enthusiasm, and explain why you want to do a PhD at all. Figure 6.3 gives an outline of a proposal that says all the right things, using a simpler style.

A good proposal makes a difference – it should be clear, precise, yet leaving room for negotiation. Most supervisors will want to help (and most students will need their help) so try not to be inflexible with your idea.

Title of Research Project
Abstract / Summary: In this research project I propose to investigate ...

Research in this area dates back to the work of ... who showed ...
Since then research has progressed, for example the work of ... who demonstrated ...
My work for my MSc project continued this theme and investigated ... resulting in a scientific paper / award / article.

This PhD addresses the clear need for further work in this area, focusing specifically on ...

<give a couple of paragraphs of detail here>

The objectives of the work are to ...
These will be achieved by ...

My interest in this area originated when ...
I find the area significant and relevant to me because ...
I would like to pursue this topic as a PhD because ...

Figure 6.3 An outline of a good PhD research proposal

A punchy summary at the beginning enables you to tell the reader exactly what they need to know at the start. A background explains existing work in the area and describes your experience and any relevant achievements. You then need to explain your idea in detail and try to describe your objectives (what the end results will be) and how you will achieve them (your research methodology – see Chapter 2). Finally, a short section explaining your interest and motivation in the topic will help convince your reader that you're serious about wanting to do a doctorate.

Very few students manage to create their PhD proposals on their own. The normal method is for you to go and talk to a potential supervisor and do a bit of brainstorming together. This means that you'll have to write several versions of your research proposal. First, you are going to have to write an initial one on your own, to attract the attention of the supervisor (as we saw in Chapter 5). After that, be prepared to work with the potential supervisor to produce modified versions that fit with each supervisor's interests that you go and meet. These may even form the basis of funding proposals submitted to a research council by your supervisor, so get this right and you might even get funding out of it.

Before you go and talk with the supervisor, you should read some of their most recent work (either find them in the library or download them from their websites). Those papers or articles will give you an idea of your shared interests. When you chat to the supervisor, you should expect to talk about how your interests match with those of the supervisor. You will also hear which of your ideas are exciting and which are out of date. It's this advice that is most important to you.

Sometimes a supervisor will think of the idea that you do for your PhD. Supervisors are more experienced and often better able to judge what will make a better project. They can listen to your interests and suggest topics that fit you and them. However, they may also have their own agendas. Many ambitious academics build themselves research groups: collections of PhD students and research assistance who all work on different aspects of a similar goal or idea. If you approach a supervisor like this, you may find it quite difficult to pursue your ideas if you decide you're more interested in a different topic.

At the end of your PhD, when you have your viva voca, the process will be rather like a negotiation. Your examiners will complain that they don't like something you've written and you will need to defend your work – negotiating a corrected version that everyone agrees with. The same process happens before you even begin. When you approach a supervisor with your idea, you need to negotiate with the supervisor: find out what they find most interesting and create a proposal that you both agree with. If you discover conflicts at this early stage then this is a pointer to future problems. Ideally you need your supervisor to be as excited as you about your research topic. Then they will encourage you and keep you going. A disinterested or bored supervisor will be of little help to you.

The final result is normally a research proposal that has emerged from discussions between the two of you. You may still have to write the document, but you can be sure that the supervisor agrees and supports the idea, and that the idea is worthy of your time and of a doctorate. It should be this document that you send with your application form.

6.3   The application form

Regardless of how well you've got to know a potential supervisor, the university will assess you based on your application form. They must ensure that you are eligible, which means you must prove that you are academically qualified and have the necessary English language skills. They need to check that you will be funded so that your fees will be paid and that you will have enough to live on. They must ensure that you have a sensible research project that is acceptable to the department. Finally, they need to allocate a primary (and often a secondary) supervisor – which will hopefully be the person or people you prefer.

Most graduate application forms follow a common format, see Figure 6.4. There are a number of important pieces of information that you will have to provide. In addition to the easy things like your name, address, academic and work background, you will be required to state that you'd like to apply for a PhD somewhere on the form[15] . You will often be asked for the title of your programme of study – this should be the title of your proposed research. You should also be able to write the name of your potential supervisor (with whom you should have met and discussed your ideas with).

Another important section of the form is the place where you specify your funding (the final page of the example given in Figure. 6.4). If you have applied (or are applying) for funding, then write that down. Note that if you list a series of extremely hard-to-get awards and your academic background is not extremely good, then the university may not believe that you'll be successful. At best that means you may be accepted, conditional on you receiving the funding. At worst, a weak list of funding options (or nothing at all) may result in your application being rejected. If you have already got funding confirmed, or you are applying for a funded studentship, or you happen to have sufficient funds, then make sure you write this down, and the university will be happy.

The final, and most important section, is listed as 'supplementary personal statement' on the example form, but may be 'research proposal'

---

[15] This may be listed as MPhil/PhD, as many universities will register you as an MPhil student initially and you'll have to transfer to full PhD registration after a year or so. If you're applying for an EngD or other form of doctorate, make sure you write its name down correctly.

or 'suggested project'. For a PhD application, you are expected to include one or more additional sheets – there won't be room on the form. It is here that you provide your own research proposal. This is the place where you demonstrate your ability to write, your interests, and your general intelligence. If you haven't found a suitable supervisor yourself, this document will be used by the department to allocate a supervisor for you.[16]

When you have filled in your form, prepared your references, gathered together all the necessary documents and submitted it all to the university, the next step is to wait for them to process it. Don't be too patient, however. Many universities have very inefficient administrative systems. If you haven't heard anything after four weeks, start calling the appropriate secretaries and chasing up the application. If this doesn't work, contact your prospective supervisor and ask for help. With luck you won't have a long wait before you receive a phone call or email setting a date for your formal interview at the university.

---

[16] Supervisor allocation is normally a voluntary process. Your application is passed to all members of staff in a department who may perform research related to the ideas in your proposal. If anyone likes the look of your application, they may say that they would be interested in supervising you. If no one is interested, you will get no supervisor, and your application will be rejected. The best way to prevent this from happening is to avoid the procedure altogether – go and talk to potential supervisors and get them to agree to supervise you before you even apply. (Of course, if you are applying for a studentship, there will be no choice about the supervisor – the academic who has the funding will supervise you.)

APPLICATION FOR ADMISSION AS A GRADUATE STUDENT

APPLICANTS ARE ADVISED TO READ THE GUIDANCE NOTES BEFORE COMPLETING THE FORM.
USE BLACK INK, BLOCK CAPITALS AND TICK BOXES AS APPROPRIATE.

PERSONAL DETAILS

FOR OFFICE USE

1. Surname / Family Name

2. First Names

3. Title (Mr/Mrs etc.)

4. Date of Birth
DAY MONTH YEAR

5. Sex
M   F

6. Nationality

7. Country of Ordinary Residence

Applic. No.

8. Home Address

9. Correspondence Address

Date of Receipt

H/O/E/X

Tel.

Fax.

Email

Tel.

Fax.

Email

Date when address is valid:

Initials

PROGRAMME OF STUDY FOR WHICH YOU WISH TO APPLY

10. Department / Institute

11. Qualification Sought (MA, Msc, etc)

12. Research Subject Area / Taught Programme Title

13. Method of Study
Full Time / Part Time

14. Proposed starting date

13. Name of proposed supervisor, if known (Mphil / PhD, MD / MS only)

Taught programmese usually start in September or early October. Research students may begin in September, January, April or July, subject to departmental approval. If there is an alternative programme for which you also wish to be considered, **you must send a photocopy of your application and all supporting papers** (except those in sealed envelopes) substituting the alternative details in this section.

FOR OFFICE USE, TO BE COMPLETED BY THE GRADUATE ADVISER/DEPARTMENTAL ADMISSIONS TUTOR AND RETURNED WILL ALL APPLICATION PAPERS TO THE ADMISSIONS OFFICE

Name of Tutor _____   Signature _____   Date_____

Departmental Action
ACCEPT / REJECT

Admissions Office to send standard letter?
YES / NO / WITHDRAWN

1. Qualification (MA, Msc, etc)

2. Research Subject Area / Taught Programme Title

3. Method of Study
Full Time / Part Time / Flexible

4. Start date

5. Research Duration

6. Principle supervisor
Full Time / Part Time / Flexible

7. Subsidiary supervisor

8. Off-campus supervisor and institute

9. Conditions of Admission
Full Time / Part Time / Flexible

11. Other information, e.g. please stipulate any studentships or scholarships allocated / nominated to be detailed on offer letter.

Figure 6.4 An example of a graduate application form

EDUCATION – QUALIFICATIONS ALREADY OBTAINED

16a. Detail your education since age 17. Start with the most recent qualifications. Where appropriate include professional qualifications.

NAME OF COLLEGE / UNIVERSITY / AWARDING BODY STATE COUNTRY IF OUTSIDE UK	START DATE	END DATE	QUALIFICATION (e.g. BA, B.Sc.)	OVERALL CLASS / GRADE / GPA	DEGREE TITLE: SUBJECTS STUDIED AND GRADES OBTAINED

EDUCATION – QUALIFICATIONS CURRENTLY BEING TAKEN

16b. Detail qualifications yet to be awarded. Where appropriate include professional qualifications.

NAME OF COLLEGE / UNIVERSITY / AWARDING BODY STATE COUNTRY IF OUTSIDE UK	START DATE	END DATE	QUALIFICATION (e.g. BA, B.Sc.)	OVERALL CLASS / GRADE / GPA	DEGREE TITLE: SUBJECTS STUDIED AND GRADES OBTAINED SO FAR

ENGLISH LANGUAGE

17. Is English your first language?

YES / NO

If "NO" detail any work experience or education that you have undertaken in English. Provide the date and grade(s) of any English language test taken. Any work experience, education or test must have been within three years of your proposed start date. A copy of the test certificate should be enclosed with this application.

FOR OFFICE USE
ADMISSIONS OFFICE ADVICE FOR THE GRADUATE ADVISOR / DEPARTMENTAL ADMISSIONS TUTOR

Academically qualified?   English language satisfactory?

YES / NOT YET / NO   YES / NO

Qualifications required / other comments:

Figure 6.4 (continued) An example of a graduate application form

EMPLOYMENT

18. List your employment to date. You may include a copy of your *curriculum vitae* if this is more convenient. Medical or dental graduates should include full details of all periods of clinical training and clinical attachments.

NAME AND ADDRESS OF EMPLOYER STATE COUNTRY IF OUTSIDE UK	START DATE	END DATE	POSITION HELD AND MAIN DUTIES

SUPPLEMENTARY PERSONAL STATEMENT

19. Describe your academic interests and reason for applying. Research (Mphil/PhD etc) applicants should state in which research areas or specific projects being offered by the department they are interested. LLM applicants should list the four subjects they wish to study. Applicants for other taught programmes, in particular flexible programmes, should indicate, where appropriate, the options/modules in which they are likely to be interested. Detail your career objectives and any relevant non-academic achievements as well as any publications. Outline any other relevant experience including attendance at specialist workshops or short courses. Continue on a separate sheet if required.

Figure 6.4 (continued) An example of a graduate application form

FUNDING

20. How will you be financing your studies?

PERSONAL OR FAMILY RESOURCES / LOAN / STUDENTSHIPS / SCHOLARSHIP / SPONSORSHIP

OTHER (PLEASE SPECIFY)

21. If you hold or are intending to apply for funding please state:

NAME OF AWARD   VALUE AND DURATION   YES / DECISION PENDING
                                                        HAS IT BEEN AWARDED?

NAME OF AWARD   VALUE AND DURATION   YES / DECISION PENDING
                                                        HAS IT BEEN AWARDED?

Please note, completion of this section does not constitute an application for funding.

AVAILABILITY FOR INTERVIEW

22. Where it is feasible, departments interview applicants before recommending admission. Overseas applicants are not normally required to attend but may be interviewed by telephone. Please indicate any periods when you might not be available.

KNOWLEDGE OF THE UNIVERSITY

23. Where did you learn about the programme applied for? Circle all those that apply.

UNIVERSITY WEBSITE / OTHER WEBSITE   PROSPECTUS / BROCHURE   ACADEMIC STAFF

EMPLOYER   FORMER GRADUATE   STUDENT FAIR / EXHIBITION   BRITISH COUNCIL

CAREERS CENTRE   NEWSPAPER / ADVERTISEMENT   OTHER:

DISABILITY / SPECIAL NEEDS

24. Do you have a disability?   YES / NO

Please also complete the disability and ethnic origin monitoring form enclosed. Any information on disability will be passed (in confidence) to the Disability Co-ordinator. If you have a disability that may require reasonable adjustments to be put in place, you must independently contact the Disability Co-ordinator to discuss your needs.

REFEREES

25. State the details of the two people who have provided references in the "Letter of Reference" envelopes that you are returning with this application

Name	Name
Position	Position
Address	Address
Tel.	Tel.
Fax.	Fax.
Email	Email

EQUAL OPPORTUNITIES POLICY

Our principle concern when considering applications is to recruit and select students who are likely to complete the programme successfully and derive benefit from it. Once these requirements are met, we regard other issues such as disability, ethnic origin, sex, marital status, number of children, beliefs relating to religion, politics and sexual orientation as irrelevant.

APPLICANT'S DECLARATION

To the best of my knowledge, the information on this application is accurate and complete. (Please note that we reserve the right to refuse admission or to terminate a student's attendance should it be discovered that he / she has made a false statement or has omitted significant information. If you are offered a place, you will be required to provide evidence of your qualifications.)

Data Protection Act 1998: I agree to the university processing personal data contained on this form, or other data wich the university may obtain from me or other people or organisations while I am applying for admission. I agree to the processing of such data for any purpose connected with my studies, or my health and safety while on UCL's premises or for any other legitimate purpose.

Signature _____   Date_____

Please return this form, together with two letters of reference, transcripts / diploma supplements, the disability and ethnic origin monitoring form and, where appropriate, and English Language certificate, to the address below.

Figure 6.4 (continued) An example of a graduate application form

7
Securing an offer

You will be invited to come for an interview once your application form has been received and is judged to be acceptable. The interview may be more of a formality if you have a supervisor on your side – but even then, if you do badly you will not be offered a place. If you are successful you will be offered a place at the university. And if you decide to accept the offer, you may then need to apply for your student visa.

7.1　The interview

So you've received a letter inviting you to come for an interview for a PhD position. You have followed the steps described previously, so you have spoken with your potential supervisor beforehand. You have also read all the material sent to you and you have thought long and hard about the research project that you would like to undertake. Funding issues should have been resolved, so you should be able to prove that both fees and living expenses will be covered for the duration of the research.

When you arrive, make sure you're wearing something smart. Academics frequently dress quite casually, even when interviewing students, but they do expect you to take the process seriously and make an effort. Go there a few minutes early, and make sure you know where to be. Most universities are like mazes inside and out, and it leaves a bad impression if you turn up late, or have to call your interviewers and tell them you're lost. The interview will usually take place in the office belonging to one of the people interviewing you, so when you enter, don't be too surprised by the sight of a messy academic's piles of books and papers nearby.

Typically, you will be interviewed by two or three members of staff. One will be the Research Students Coordinator (also sometimes called the

Admissions Tutor, or Research Students Administrator). Academics normally have to do administrative jobs as well as teaching and research, so this person might be a lecturer or a professor. He or she will be asking the difficult questions, to make sure you know what you're letting yourself in for. Another interviewer will be your potential supervisor – who will be on your side if you have already spoken to him or her and built up a rapport. The supervisor will often ask more technical questions, to make sure that you are capable of performing the research you'd like to do. Sometimes there is an additional administrator, or perhaps a Research Fellow or Research Assistant on an existing project, with whom you might work. They often play a minor role in the interview.

If you are an 'insider' and have completed an MSc or BSc in the same department, then you will be known to staff and the interview will be more of a formality. If you have your own guaranteed funding (and this does not include your parents or your savings), then the interview will also be relatively straightforward. But if you have applied for a studentship then you may be competing with many other candidates for the same position, and the interview will be tougher (indeed, you might have more than one interview). If you have no funding, if your research idea is badly thought out or non-existent, or if you have no idea what PhD research is all about, then you may find that you fail the interview completely and are not offered a PhD place.

Your manner will be assessed during the interview: how confident you are, whether you can communicate effectively, and how intelligent you are. It's normal to be nervous, so don't worry about that. But do try to speak confidently and clearly. Try not to ramble. Most importantly, *listen carefully* to the question you are being asked, and try to answer it. If you don't understand the question, say so, and ask for clarification. If English is not your first language and you have trouble understanding or being understood, just take your time and don't panic. Academics work with international students all the time and are quite used to dealing with a few misunderstandings. They can also tell the difference between someone who is very bright but temporarily lost for words and someone who is not bright enough to do a doctorate. But do try to answer the question asked of you. If you keep diverging from the subject that your interviewers are trying to explore, you will frustrate them and even make them suspicious.

In one memorable interview I performed with a student, I asked what I thought was a quite innocuous question about the candidate's CV. He had done an undergraduate degree and a Masters, but there seemed to be several years unaccounted for, so I asked him what he had done in that time. The response was very strange – the candidate rambled for several minutes and avoided answering the question. I continued asking the same question, now wondering what was going on. Eventually it emerged that the candidate had spent some of the time doing a second Masters degree – for some reason he thought it would look bad if he admitted this. Alerted to this strange behaviour, I continued to study his CV and realized that there was still some time unaccounted for. After some pressing, it turned out that the candidate had spent that time doing a third Masters degree! Now, you cannot be overqualified to do a PhD (indeed some people who already have a PhD apply to do another). But being dishonest in your interview, or trying to hide information about yourself, is usually disastrous. The interviewers are left wondering what they can believe, and if you cannot trust a student, the risks are too great to accept them for a PhD – which is what happened to that candidate.

If you are confident that you can do a PhD and already have a clear idea of what you want to do, that's great. But be warned – your interviewers will almost certainly know more than you do about everything you talk about during the interview. They'll know exactly what a PhD entails, what kind of person can do a PhD, what technical problems you are likely to face in your chosen area, and they'll know about you from the references they've obtained. Confidence is great, cockiness is not. A cocky candidate may not be able to listen and learn effectively during their research, so however confident you are, do convey a certain level of deference towards your interviewers.

Here's a list of questions commonly asked during the interview. You might find it useful to think about how you would answer each one.

Why do you think you'd like to do a PhD?
What do you think a PhD entails?
What do you think are the best and worst parts about doing a PhD?
Why do you think you are suited to do a PhD?
So you're interested in X. Tell me what you've done in the area and what you'd like to do for your PhD.
Let's say you design and create something during the course of your research, but even though you try very hard you can't make it work. What will you do?
You haven't qualified for our studentship place; how are you going to pay the tuition fees and cover your living expenses?
What attracted you to our university?

Perhaps the best way to learn how best to do a PhD interview is to 'listen in' on a couple of them. Here are two PhD interviews (for a science-based PhD) based on questions and answers given by real interviewers and candidates, to give you a better idea of how you can answer the questions. Let's begin with an example of how *not* to do it. Everyone has shaken hands and sat down, and the questions begin:

Admissions Tutor:	I'd like to start by asking why you think you'd like to do a PhD.
Interviewee:	Uh, I don't know really. I finished my degree and looked for a job, but couldn't find anything good. Then I saw an advert for PhDs here and thought I'd have a go.
Admissions Tutor:	What do you think a PhD entails?
Interviewee:	Oh, it's kinda like my undergrad degree project, only longer, I think.
Admissions Tutor:	What do you think are the best and worst parts about doing a PhD?
Interviewee:	Um, the best parts are being able to lie in late ... and the worst parts are maybe not getting enough money.
Admissions Tutor:	Why do you think you are suited to do a PhD?
Interviewee:	Uh, I dunno. I'm here, aren't I?
Supervisor:	So you're interested in X. Tell me what you've done in the area and what you'd like to do for your PhD.
Interviewee:	I did X for my degree project; I did what my supervisor told me to. I just put that subject down on the form as I couldn't think of anything else.
Supervisor:	Let's say you design and create something during the course of your research, but even though you try very hard you can't make it work. What will you do?
Interviewee:	Um, I guess I'd fail then?
Admissions Tutor:	You haven't qualified for our studentship place; how are you going to pay the tuition fees and cover your living expenses?
Interviewee:	You mean I have to pay you?
Supervisor:	What attracted you to our university?
Interviewee:	My girlfriend has got a job nearby.

Rather obviously, this candidate would not be successful. Every question was answered in a way that would ring alarm bells in the minds of the interviewers. The potential student clearly has little idea what a PhD is, and will be highly unlikely to have the motivation necessary to gain a doctorate. Here's how you should do it:

Admissions Tutor:	I'd like to start by asking why you think you'd like to do a PhD.
Interviewee:	It's something I've wanted to do for as long as I've known about it. I almost feel driven to do this – I can't think of anything else I'd rather do right now.
Admissions Tutor:	What do you think a PhD entails?
Interviewee:	A lot of hard work. I've spoken with PhD students and I know research can be difficult and it won't always go the way I want it to. I know I'll have to learn a bunch of new skills like public speaking, designing experiments and scientific writing. But I think I can do it.
Admissions Tutor:	What do you think are the best and worst parts about doing a PhD?
Interviewee:	The best part is following my interests, satisfying my hunger for knowledge. The worst part is probably depression when it doesn't go to plan. But I think I'm very motivated and will get through those difficult times.
Admissions Tutor:	Why do you think you are suited to do a PhD?
Interviewee:	I think I have the right kind of personality: a love of research, an ability to focus on a problem, and enormous motivation and stubbornness to see me through to the end.
Supervisor:	So you're interested in X. Tell me what you've done in the area and what you'd like to do for your PhD.
Interviewee:	I've been interested in X for a long time. I did my degree project on the topic which resulted in a conference paper, and since then I've continued working on it in my spare time.
Supervisor:	Let's say you design and create something during the course of your research, but even though you try very hard you can't make it work. What will you do?
Interviewee:	Well, I think the point of science is to understand and gain knowledge. As long as new knowledge is learned from the work, I don't think it can be called a failure.
Admissions Tutor:	You haven't qualified for our studentship place; how are you going to pay the tuition fees and cover your living expenses?

Interviewee:	I have been awarded a grant from Y, which will pay the fees and living expenses.
Supervisor:	What attracted you to our university?
Interviewee:	I have looked around and I think your department and university are doing exactly the kind of work I'm interested in.

This is the kind of candidate that leaves a confident, happy feeling with the interviewers. The potential student has clearly done a lot of homework and is making a sensible choice for their future. Those answers that indicate an awareness of PhDs show that this person is strongly motivated and very likely to achieve the doctorate.

Ultimately, this is the point of interviewing you. The university needs to make sure you will be able to get a doctorate. They need to assess whether you have the motivation, the imagination, and the funds to see you through. Your supervisor has to make a commitment of at least three years of her time, so she wants to make sure you'll be worth the effort. She will be working closely with you, so she will also want to make sure you will get along. If the university is providing funding, then they will want to make sure that you don't waste the money. If you give up after a year, you will still have spent a year's money, making it very difficult for the university to find someone to replace you – they will not have enough money for the new student.

The example questions and answers given above are just that – examples. Don't try to learn your answers from them, because your interviewers will ask other questions and will be able to tell if you are not being sincere. (They might also have read this book!) If you find that your answers are more similar to the first candidate's response than the second candidate's, you should think seriously about whether a PhD is the right thing for you to do at this point in your life.

But assuming things have gone well, at the end of the interview you may be given a chance to ask questions of your own. Do take the opportunity if you have anything you are not sure about. It's often a good time to ask about where you would work, what kind of support is provided for conference trips, what kind of equipment you would be given for your own use, what paperwork or assessment needs to be done now and during the course of the research, and whether you are expected to do courses or teaching. Any technical questions about the project can wait until you and your supervisor are alone.

It is possible that you will be told at the end of the interview that you will be offered a place at the university. This usually happens when the interview is more of a formality. But if you are competing for a PhD studentship place, you may not hear anything for several days or even a couple of weeks. Don't worry – if you are successful, you will be told the outcome. If it takes a while, don't go and pester your potential supervisor for a result – you're more likely to irritate than anything else. If you are not successful, don't worry. It takes most students several attempts before they are offered a place they are satisfied with.

If you've been accepted, congratulations! But remember that this is the first of several such interviews, often performed yearly, or at the 9-month and 18-month stages, culminating in the viva voca – the defence of your PhD thesis. At each stage, the questions will get harder and more technical. But once you've been accepted for a PhD place, the objective of the staff at your new university is just one thing – to help you get a doctorate, whatever it takes.

7.2 The offer

Following a successful interview with an eligible student, most universities will offer a conditional PhD place. The conditions you have to satisfy are eligibility and monetary. If you are waiting for your undergraduate or MSc results, the place may be conditional on you achieving the degree. But all PhD positions require that fees are paid before you can begin.

A studentship is normally a fully-funded position, so your acceptance means that the fees will be paid, and it's all systems go! Otherwise, you must make sure your funding is secured and goes through to the university (or that you pay it yourself) before you can become enrolled as a student with the university.

Figure 7.1 gives an example of a real acceptance letter. In the example, the foreign student has done her homework and already provided evidence that she is eligible and she can pay the fees, as well as her application form and two references, so the offer is unconditional. Such a letter may be accompanied by a reply form, enrolment forms, details of the fees due, university regulations and possibly details of university accommodation. Once she has read everything carefully and made up her mind, she would return the reply form telling the college that she accepts the offer, fill out the student enrolment forms and pay the first set of fees (or ensure her funding has paid for them). She then just has to find somewhere nearby to live, and she can begin her doctorate.

Note that, if you have applied for a PhD, it is common practice to be offered an MPhil place first. After between 12 and 30 months (depending on the university), you will transfer your registration to that of full PhD student, once you can demonstrate suitable ability and a sensible research programme.

7 June 2006   Reference: 21200841/1

Dear Miss Hopeful

FORMAL OFFER OF ADMISSION

I am pleased to inform you that the College is offering you a place on the MPhil/PhD programme with effect from 1 August 2006. You have been accepted to undertake full-time research for an MPhil/PhD in Biology under the supervision of Prof White and a second supervisor yet to be appointed, the area of your research being 'Innate immunity interactions with T-cells'.

The normal length of study for a PhD is three years full-time or five years part-time. Full-time students are expected to be available for supervision and other directed research training for at least 21 hours a week on average in term time. Part-time students will not normally be required to spend more than 20 hours per week on average on their studies. Please bear this in mind when making arrangements for your studies, and read this letter carefully to ensure that you fully understand the conditions under which you are being accepted. Included with this letter is a summary of the Postgraduate Training and Research for the MPhil and PhD degrees: College Code of Practice, the full version of which is on the College website. You are strongly advised to read the full version before you reply to this offer.

The offer is made subject to the following conditions (any that you have already satisfied will be indicated):

Pre-Enrolment

Enrolment papers will be sent to you from June onwards or as soon as you have fulfilled any outstanding pre-enrolment conditions.

Unconditional offer

End of conditions

We have received a satisfactory reference from your first referee.

We have received a satisfactory reference from your second referee.

Post-Enrolment (these must be completed by 31 July)

If you have not already done so, please forward evidence that you have satisfied these conditions as soon as this is available.

Thank you for providing your registration documentation.

Thank you for providing us with your degree transcript.

Fees Classification:

You have been classified as an overseas student for fees purposes.

Fees for the 2006/2007 session are enclosed for information.

Fee details are posted on the College website from 1May.

This offer is made on the basis of the information that you have supplied in your application form. If any of this information is found to be inaccurate, the offer will be rendered null and void.

If you wish to accept this offer and its conditions, please complete the enclosed reply form and return it to the Registry within two weeks of the date of this letter.

If you need to communicate with us about your application, please include your name and reference number as it appears in this letter, together with the title of the programme as it given above. This will help us to deal with your query more quickly. Please contact Registry on the phone number or email above.

We look forward to hearing from you.

Yours sincerely,

Registrar

Figure 7.1 An example of a PhD offer letter sent to a successful applicant.

Just make sure it is what you want. You do not have to accept an offer immediately, although you may be under pressure to give an answer within a few days. If you haven't checked out details of the university, supervisor and research project already, now is the time to do so. If you don't feel comfortable with anything, try to talk it through with your supervisor. You do not have to accept any offer – but if you choose to reject it (perhaps because you also received a better offer from somewhere else), then be quick about letting them know. You don't want a supervisor and his department to do a lot of work, perhaps including the allocation of funding for you, only for you to tell them at the last minute that you have changed your mind. Annoying people (who might one day become your colleagues) is not a great start to a research career.

Even if you are offered a PhD studentship and accept it, you can still change your mind (just as you can quit the PhD at any time once you have started). However, the repercussions for others are even worse if you do this. When you accept a studentship, the funds are allocated to you. All the other candidates are notified that they have been unsuccessful. If you then tell the university that you've changed your mind, they might have to readvertise the position, reinterview, and sort out all the paperwork for the funds again. That will involve quite a bit of time and cost. If you quit after you've actually enrolled in the university, it is likely that some of the funding will have been spent on the fees for your first term. This means there may not be enough left for another student and you could cause a lot of problems for the supervisor and university.

You must always make the decision that is right for you. If you've been following the advice in this book, you will have checked things out beforehand so that you will not have to put anyone in a difficult situation. In the end, you have to do the work, so make sure it is what you want to do before you agree.

7.3   Student visas

If you have accepted your offer, you then need to satisfy all the conditions – finish the existing degree, obtain funding, provide references – and provide evidence to the administration of the university. They will send you your unconditional offer, like the one shown in Figure 7.1. If you are an international student, you must now apply for your student visa.

A visa is an official document that you present with your passport at Immigration Control in order to be granted entry into the UK. Thankfully, in recent years, the process of obtaining a visa has been streamlined and targets have been put into place to speed up visa processing. However, the bad news is that visa fees are getting more and more expensive. EU citizens generally do not require visas. Note that the specific visa requirements for your country will be listed on the UK government information leaflets and websites – see the resources section at the end of the book for more details.

There are two ways in which you can apply for a student visa. First, you can apply in your own country, either by downloading the online forms or by going in person to a British Embassy, Consulate or High Commission in your country. Second, you can enter the UK as a 'prospective student' (you'll still need to complete the appropriate entry paperwork and inform the Immigration Officer of this status when you arrive). This gives you six months to stay in the UK while you sort out your PhD course, and you should apply for your student visa during this time. Note that, from experience, it is usually considerably cheaper, quicker (and sometimes mandatory) to apply for your student visa in your own country.

You have to satisfy several important conditions before you get yourself a student visa. If you follow the advice in this book, these should not be difficult to achieve, but be warned – political climates can change without warning, so it is conceivable you may be refused entry into the UK. If in doubt, check with the British Embassy *before* you attempt to travel.

To qualify for a student visa you must ensure that:

- You have an *unconditional* offer of a PhD place at a university. To prove this, you'll need your acceptance letter from your university. This must be an official letter from the university – do not try to use anything else or you may find your application rejected, and possibly you might be on the next flight home.
- The PhD is full-time (specifically, that it involves more than 15 hours per week of study).
- You can prove that you will be able to cover the cost of your fees and living expenses during your stay, without needing to work or rely on state benefits. To do this, you have to provide details of the university fees for the PhD you will be doing. Your university will send you details of these in a letter, or they will be online. You will also have to provide accurate details of any funding you will receive (with an official letter from the funder) or details of your bank statements, or the statements of a relative who has agreed to fund your studies (with a letter from them confirming this). If you plan to rely on part-time work to pay for some of your costs, this work must be at the university or institute where you will study and it must be guaranteed by them, in writing. Even so, this may not be taken into account, so is a dangerous course of action.
- You intend to leave the UK on completion of the course. (Note that this will not stop you from applying for a work visa and working in the UK after you finish, but to get a student visa you must *say* that you intend to leave when you're done.)

Generally, a UK student visa application will need the following documents:

- your passport;
- two recent passport-sized photographs (these must of the correct size and may need to be signed on the reverse by someone to prove the likeness of you);
- the visa fee, which is non-refundable;
- any relevant diplomas or educational certificates which you hold;
- a letter from the university, college or school confirming your acceptance for the course of study in the UK and a statement of charges for the course;
- evidence of government/industrial sponsorship (if appropriate), or evidence of support from elsewhere, or evidence that your own finances are sufficient to cover all the costs;

Some applicants also include references or statements from the PhD supervisor or funders, providing confirmation of their acceptance, details of the PhD course and confirmation of the fees and funding. You may well be invited for an interview during which you will be asked to confirm all of the above details. They will be checking that you are not pretending to be a student in order to gain illegal entry into the UK. Be honest and prepare well and you should have no problems.

Because PhDs do not always follow the standard term times, your student visa may be dated until 31 October following the proposed end of the doctorate or 4 months after the end of the doctorate. However, don't be too surprised if your first student visa is only valid for one year or 18 months. This is not uncommon – you'll just need to renew it before it runs out.

Even though you must be a full-time student to receive a student visa, you are allowed to work in the UK. At the time of writing, international students with student visas may work '20 hours per week during term time and 40 hours per week during holidays'. Your spouse or children may be able to work without restrictions if you are studying longer than one year.

8
Accommodation

Your living environment is very important. You may work from home at least some of the time and you need to make sure you're happy and safe, or your work will suffer. If you are planning to do a part-time doctorate, or you've managed to get a place in the local university so you don't need to move, that's great. But it's more likely that you'll be starting not just a new working life, but also dealing with a new home, and possibly even a new country.

8.1   What do you need?

Most PhDs are not like undergraduate or Masters degrees. Although you may have a taught element to begin with, it will not be long before you begin to specialize in your chosen area. After a couple of years, your focus will be sufficiently narrow that only a very small number of people in the world may fully appreciate what you are doing. Those people should include your supervisor, and if you're lucky, may include one or two of your colleagues in the same group. But you may find that your true peers are spread across the world and you may only meet them at occasional conferences or exhibitions. This makes a PhD quite a lonely thing to do – very different from the shared experiences of undergraduate or MSc degrees – so it's a good idea to live in a place where you won't be too isolated from friendly faces.

There can be other unfortunate side effects of doing your PhD. You will make many new friends, which is great, but you may find that some of your older friends struggle to come to terms with your new life. They may not understand why a PhD is so important to you; they may strive to convince themselves and others that you're just avoiding a 'real job'; they may even become so jealous of who you become that you lose them as friends altogether. Although this is sad, it is not uncommon. You will grow as a person in many ways: intellectually, in confidence, in analysis and communication. Your true friends will be happy for you. Nevertheless, you will find that living with old friends who are not doing a PhD may not be a long-term solution.

And then there is your time. At the start of their PhD, every student thinks they have eternity. Plenty of time for fun and sleeping late. But it doesn't take long for most to realize that this is going to be hard work, and after the first 18 months fly by, most students start to think that three or four years is not going to be enough time. The hours get longer, weekends become useful extra time to do work. Evenings are handy quiet times when you can think. So sharing a house with undergraduates, however fun and entertaining they are, may not work. You are not going to have the time to go to all the parties you once went to. You might find that you need some time alone to concentrate. It's very difficult to write a 200-page thesis in a noisy, bustling environment.

8.2 Budgets

Unless you are lucky enough to be rich or have a fabulous source of funding, another three or four years of being a student and coping with expensive UK prices will mean that you should be careful with your money. If you are new to the UK, this is very important – it's remarkably easy to find yourself tens of thousands of pounds in the red. You can achieve that in a couple of years. It may take you ten times as long to pay it all back.

Your accommodation is likely to be the most expensive cost you will incur. So it is vital that you budget properly for your PhD. Work out how much money you have got each month – and assume that you will take a year longer than you envisage. UK PhD students are permitted to work part-time (20 hours per week during term time, 40 hours per week outside term time), and it is common for them to take small paid jobs in laboratories or give tutorials. The money you receive from such work is a bonus – you must not rely on work to pay your fees or any of your bills (indeed, there are student visa restrictions for foreign students stating this explicitly). You will need money for your rent, for travel to and from the university and trips home to see friends and family, food, and for other bills. Don't just make up the numbers, do some research and find out how much things cost. In the UK, even the cost of food will vary dramatically depending on your location. As a rule, London (or other large cities) are much more expensive than smaller towns. The south of England is more expensive than the north (and Scotland and Northern Ireland). London is one of the most expensive cities in the world.

Your budget will affect the quality of the room or apartment you live in, and its location. It is important not to overstretch yourself financially when you choose your accommodation. Equally, don't just pick the cheapest. There will be a good reason why it is cheap: usually it will be rather unpleasant inside, very small, or in a dangerous part of town. I write from experience – my own PhD was significantly coloured by my poor choice of accommodation, which although cheap and nice inside, was in a very bad part of town. Three years of witnessing crimes, being threatened, burgled and giving police reports does not make it easy to concentrate on your research. The only plus side about living somewhere that you hate is that it really makes you finish the doctorate very quickly – just so you can leave!

Remember to prioritize your bills – paying the rent is more important than a wonderfully full social life. Indeed, you might not be able to afford all the evenings in the pubs that younger students enjoy. As an extreme example, it is the custom in England to buy a 'round' of drinks for everyone when in a group. If you were with six people and went to a nice London bar, an evening could easily cost you £100. If you also went for a meal, went clubbing, or went to the theatre, it might be £150 or £200. Do that kind of thing a couple of times a week and you will spend over £10,000 a year. (If sterling is not your currency, then work it out – it's enough to buy a house in some countries.)

In some cultures it is unusual for men to cook their own meals. They come to England and expect to live by buying all their meals in restaurants or from takeaways. And then they arrive and receive a shock. A cheap takeaway meal is rarely less than £5; a full restaurant meal may be £40. Within a week, they find they have spent their entire month's money on food. I once heard of a student becoming so desperate that he used to buy seven hamburgers from a fast-food chain on a Friday (when there was always a special offer) and freeze them, cooking a new one in the microwave for dinner each day. Don't do that. The lesson is clear – when ingredients for a good, healthy meal may be only £1, you need to learn how to cook before you come. Getting into debt just because you cannot be bothered to cook is plain stupid.

Of course, if you are thinking of paying for your own student fees without any funding, you may be heavily in debt already. Just don't let the numbers fool you. Yes, you may be expecting to be £20,000 in the red. But £30,000 or £40,000 is *much* worse! One of the most common reasons why PhD students quit, or never get around to writing their thesis is lack of money. Don't be one of them. Plan ahead.

8.3   University accommodation

Once you know what you can afford for accommodation, your options will depend on your status. An overseas student, parent, or married student may qualify for university accommodation, at least for the first year. If you are very lucky that might mean you get your own small apartment (usually these are reserved for married couples or those with children). But most UK universities are very short of space and so the best you'll get is a room in the 'halls' – large, often rather primitive and dilapidated buildings filled with little bedrooms, shared bathrooms and kitchens. Sometimes there are no kitchens at all – the university provides cooked meals in a canteen. Make sure you can eat the kind of traditional and sometimes unimaginative food they serve (in England, a dinner may comprise dishes such as lasagne, chilli con carne, steak and kidney pie, chicken curry, or the favourite on Fridays: fish and chips).

It is not easy to secure university accommodation. There are often waiting lists, so you may need to apply for your room as soon as you have accepted your PhD offer. If you have children, make sure you check that there are nursery facilities and space for them during the day. All universities have accommodation offices or departments with people there to help you. Some even have extensive websites allowing you to browse the options online. You should be given information about accommodation in the material you receive with your acceptance letter. If not, your supervisor (or even just the university switchboard or website) will be able to give you the phone number to call. Be warned, it can be a frustrating process, for you may not find out where your room will be until they allocate it – and they may not do that until just before you start. Whether you choose to wait and see will probably depend on how confident you are about living in private accommodation, cooking your own meals and looking after yourself.

Universities based in cities may have their student halls spread across a wide area. Some halls may be lovely, while others might be pretty nasty. You may find some are very convenient for the university, while others involve a 40-minute commute. You may also find that some are in areas that are not very safe. Sadly, student accommodation usually means cheap accommodation, which also means you might be in the cheaper, rougher part of town. It's definitely worth going and having a look around the halls where you might be staying. Go two or three times, at different times of day, to get a feel for the area. This could be your home for several years, so take this seriously. Examples of city universities like these are: all London-based universities, the Universities of Nottingham, Leeds, Birmingham, Edinburgh (and many others).

Campus-based universities are a little different. These are like sprawling little towns, often some distance from the city or town they are associated with. They have custom-built accommodation on site, shops, banks and everything you need (yes, bars, too). Some students spend their whole time on campus, working, socializing, shopping and sleeping. The environment is usually very safe, although the choice of accommodation may be very limited. It is more common for postgraduate students (especially UK citizens) to live in private accommodation near to the campus, but not actually on it. Examples of campus universities like these are: the University of Essex, the University of Sussex, the University of Kent, the University of Bath (and many others).

8.4   Private accommodation

Many PhD students prefer to find a room in a shared house or flat. This is often an ideal solution – you have a little more privacy, you may make some close friends with your flatmates, and you may have a little more space. Sharing with young professionals can be a good option. They are less likely to have problems paying their share of the bills and are often mature enough to deal with the fact you're studying to become a doctor. But sharing with fellow PhD students is usually the best solution. You can learn from their experiences, give each other advice, and discover that the highs and lows you experience are completely normal for all PhD students.

Although it may be tempting to share a house with people who all come from the same country as you, or speak the same language, it will actually be extremely beneficial if you can share with people from several backgrounds. If you are English it will broaden your experience of other cultures, you'll probably have some tasty new food to try and you may learn new languages. If you are not English, then you will find your spoken English will improve dramatically by living among native English speakers for a while.

You can find shared houses and apartments advertised in most university unions on their noticeboards, and their accommodation offices will be able to assist you with current availabilities. You will also find private accommodation advertised in newspapers such as *Loot* (although in London the rooms are let so quickly that you typically have to buy the paper early in the morning, ring as many numbers as you can and spend the day viewing them, being prepared to say 'yes' and pay a deposit on the spot).

The problem with private accommodation is that you are outside the university system, so when things go wrong, you have to sort them out for yourself. When looking for a house- or flat-share, you need to be careful. Not all landlords know what they are doing, and many do not obey the UK housing regulations. For example, in recent years, a new kind of landlord has emerged. These dodgy characters will let out each room of a house or flat separately. They will turn every room (except the kitchen and bathroom) into a bedroom, and some even divide up the larger rooms to make more, smaller rooms. In London I once visited what was supposed to be three-bedroom apartment, which had been turned into a seven-bedroom warren. Such living spaces can be unpleasant because you have no living room to relax or socialize in, and the load on the kitchen and bathroom means that they are perpetually filthy and in use. The other bad thing is that you have no control over whom you live with. The landlord is free to accept anyone at any time into the other rooms, so you may end up living with some very strange people.

Another common source of problems can be the live-in landlord. If you act as a lodger in someone else's house or apartment, the relationship can be unequal. You may find your privacy is invaded because the owner believes he or she has the right to go into any room at any time. You might find the rent goes up when the landlord is short of money. You might find it very difficult to convince the landlord that a wall needs repainting or a carpet replacing – if he can live with the peeling paint and mould, why are you complaining? Or you may be asked to leave the house sometimes to give the landlord some privacy. (The landlord does not have the right to do any of these things, but it may not stop him.)

Usually the best solution is to team up with a group of fellow PhD students and rent a flat or house together. If you are all students, then you won't have to pay council tax (a regional tax used to pay for local amenities such as waste collection, police and schools in the UK), which will reduce everyone's bills. (Strictly speaking, even if you are a student sharing with professionals, you should not pay any council tax. You may not be very popular with the other residents who will have to pay, though.)

When you are looking, do check the area, your flatmates and the landlord, as well as the property. Make sure you visit the property at different times of day and try out the journey from there to the university. Whoever you share with (whether they are a stranger or your sibling), make sure they sign a contract committing them to pay their share of the bills. Arguments about money will always happen, but if everyone has signed a contract, at least it should be clear who is supposed to pay what. Checking out the landlord may be more difficult. Talking to the previous tenants is a very good idea. They will be able to tell you if the landlord promised to repaint the walls, re-tile the bathroom and replace the carpets when they moved in, and that he never did any of it. If the landlord demands the rent in cash, then he is probably dodging the income tax he should pay (a very common trick, but illegal with a possible prison sentence if he is caught). It is also not safe for you to be withdrawing large amounts of cash each month – the casual thief loves a nice brown envelope or fat wallet on its way to the landlord. (Also make sure you always get a signed receipt for every payment you make.) A good landlord will always accept a cheque, although he may wait until it's cleared before you can move in.

If the landlord does not provide a proper contract to sign, this is also bad news. I once saw what was described as a rental agreement, scrawled in three lines on the back of an envelope in ungrammatical and mis-spelled English. If anything went wrong, such a 'document' would be worthless and would not protect you or the landlord. Figure 8.1 gives a real tenancy agreement, which you can copy and use if you wish. As you can see, it is a detailed legal document (in the UK), outlining your responsibilities and the responsibilities of the landlord. It should be signed by you and the landlord and also by a witness (to prove it was not signed under duress). You should be given a copy to keep.

Once you and everyone else sharing the accommodation has signed the agreement, do make sure a clear inventory and record are made of all items and their state of repair. If you have a camera, take photos of your room and all areas you will use before you move in, focusing on anything that looks dirty or damaged. You will have to pay the landlord a large deposit in addition to the first month's rent. If you want to see all of the deposit back when you leave, you will need proof that you are leaving everything in the same condition as you found it. Again, I write from experience – I once rented an apartment from a lovely woman with whom I got on very well. But when I left, she still charged me to have some stained kitchen appliances professionally cleaned. I didn't have the photographs to prove that the stains had been there when I'd moved in, so I lost the money.

Finally, if you are sharing, make sure everybody knows the house rules. In addition to paying their share of the bills, you need to make sure everyone agrees to doing their share of the cleaning, does not disturb you, and doesn't leave garbage or dirty dishes lying around the place. You may also need to make it clear who owns different items of food, perhaps by each having your own storage area in the kitchen. When you're struggling with money, it's not nice to find someone else has eaten your food without asking.

Sharing student accommodation can be an enjoyable and fun experience, which will assist you during your doctorate, and may result in some life-long friends.

AN AGREEMENT FOR LETTING FURNISHED DWELLING HOUSE ON AN ASSURED
SHORTHOLD TENANCY UNDER THE HOUSING ACT 1988 AS AMENDED

THIS TENANCY AGREEMENT is made the _____[1] day of _____[2] Two Thousand and _____[3]
BETWEEN _____[4]
of _____
_____[5] (hereinafter called 'The Landlord')
and _____[6]
of _____
_____[7] (hereinafter called 'The Tenant')
IT IS AGREED as follows
1 THE LANDLORD LETS AND THE TENANT TAKE all that property known as

_____[8] (hereinafter called 'The Premises')
TOGETHER WITH the fixtures and fittings and furniture and effects herein listed on the
inventory attached hereto FOR A TERM commencing on the _____[9] day of _____[10] Two
Thousand and _____[11] and terminating on the _____[12] day of _____[13] Two Thousand and
_____[14] as an Assured Shorthold Tenancy subject to the provisions Part 1 of the Housing
Act 1988
The Tenants agree to pay a rent of £_____[14]
exclusive of _____[15]
and inclusive of _____[16]
for every month/week[17] of the said term without any deductions whatsoever on the _____[18]
day of each month/week[17] the first of such payments to be made on the signing hereof.
On the granting of the Tenancy the Tenants shall deposit the sum of £_____[19] with the
Landlord or Agent to be held by them until the expiration of the Tenancy against
dilapidations or charges found to have accrued during the Tenacy which deposit will be
returned in full or less any deductions deemed necessary after the expiration of the Tenacy
2 THIS AGREEMENT is intended to create an Assured Shorthold Tenancy as defined in
   Section 20 of the Housing Act 1988 and the provisions for the recovery of possession by
   the Landlord in Section 21 thereof applying accordingly.
3 THE TENANTS AGREE WITH THE LANDLORD as follows
  (i)   to pay the said rent and any additional fees provided said fees are agreed at the time of
        signing this document
  (ii) Not to make any structural changes or cause damage beyond normal wear and tear or
        share sell sublet or loan any decoration or items listed in the inventory and to accept
        deduction from the deposit for the cleaning repair or replacement costs of any such
        change loss or damage at the end of the Tenancy as determined by the Landlord
  (iii) To permit the Landlord or Agent of the Landlord with or without workmen and others
        at all reasonable times during the Tenancy by prior appointment (unless the situation
        demands emergency access) to enter the Premises for the purposes of repairing painting
        or other necessary repairs or examining the state and condition of the premises or
        enabling future tenants to view the Premises and the persons so entering causing as
        little inconvenience disturbance and damage as possible and making good all damage
  (iv) Not to cause nuisance through

        _____[20]
  (v)   To ensure the following are maintained in good order
        _____[21]

4 IT IS HEREBY DECLARED that such aforesaid covenants shall remain in full force both at
   Law and in equity notwithstanding that the Landlord shall have waived or released
   temporarily or permanently revocably or irrevocably or otherwise

*Figure 8.1 A typical tenancy agreement, which is legally binding in the UK, with
all the details you need in it to protect you and the landlord*

5 PROVIDED THAT if the rent or any instalment shall be in arrears or unpaid for at least
____[22] days after the same shall have become due or if there shall be a breach of any of
the agreements on the part of the Tenants herein contained then the Landlord may
re-enter upon and take possession.
6 THE LANDLORD AGREES WITH THE TENANTS as follows
  (i) to pay all taxes fees and other costs due to a Superior Landlord and insure and keep insured
the Premises and the Landlord's furniture fixtures and effects in their full replacement value
and to return to the Tenants any and all necessary rent to compensate damage or unusable
items or uninhabitable property covered by said insurance
  (ii) to keep in good repair and properly working order the heating electrical appliances and
other equipment provided by the Landlord for the use of the Tenants (unless such repair is
necessary as a result of damage sustained through misuse by the Tenants)
  (iii) that the Tenants paying the rent and performing the agreement on the part of the Tenants
herein contained may quietly possess and enjoy the premises during the Tenancy without
any lawful interruption from the Landlord or any person under or in trust for the Landlord
or by title paramount
7 IN THIS AGREEMENT WHERE THE CONTEXT SO ADMITS where there are two or more persons included in the expression 'The Tenant' convenances expressed to be made by the Tenant shall be deemed to be made by such persons jointly and severally
8 THE TENANTS AND OCCUPANTS SHALL FORTHWITH REGISTER for the council tax with
the local authority and ensure all other taxes and licenses not payable by the Landlord are
promptly paid
9 IT IS HEREBY AGREED THAT if either party wish to terminate this agreement at any time after
the expiration of the first ____[23] months they can do so by giving to the other party ____[24]
clear weeks previous written notice at which time this agreement will cease without prejudice
to the rights remedies of either party in respect of any previous claim
10 INVENTORY as appears attached hereto marked 'A'
11 THIS AGREEMENT shall take effect subject to the provisions of Section 11 of the Landlord and
Tenant Act 1985 applicable to the Tenancy

Tenant	[25]	Date	[26]
Landlord	[27]	Date	[28]
Witness	[29]	Date	[30]

---

[1] Day, [2] Month and [3] Year Tenancy agreement begins
[4] Landlord's full name [5] Landlord's address or contact telephone number
[6] Your full name [7] Your home or previous address and a contact telephone number
[8] The full address of the rental property
[9] Day, [10] Month and [11] Year you can move in
[12] Day, [13] Month and [14] Year you must move out (you need to sign a new document
renewing this agreement for another term if you wish to stay longer).
[14] The rent you must pay, exclusive of [15] bills (e.g. electricity and phone), inclusive of [16] bills
(e.g. water rates and gas). These are determined by the Landlord.
[17] Delete as appropriate (are you paying monthly or weekly?) [18] day of month/week you must
pay.
[19] Security deposit to be held by the Landlord and returned at the end of the Tenancy (often
between 1 and 2 times the monthly rent).
[20] Landlord's prohibition rules (e.g. owning pets, making excessive noise, leaving untidy
garbage)
[21] Other aspects you must maintain (e.g., garden, shed, garage)
[22] Number of days in arrears before the Landlord can cancel the agreement (typically 21).
[23] Number of months before you can cancel the agreement (often 6).
[24] Number of weeks notice you have to give before you leave (often 8 weeks or 2 months).
[25] Your signature and [26] date, [27] Landlord's signature and [28] date, [29] Signature of a witness
and [30] date

---

*Figure 8.1 (continued) A typical tenancy agreement, which is legally binding in
the UK, with all the details you need in it to protect you and the landlord*

9
Beginning your PhD

The easy part is over – you've got yourself a PhD place in a university you like, a good supervisor, a project you believe in, a nice place to live and hopefully some funding to pay for it all. Now comes the hard part. You've got to get yourself a PhD. To finish your journey towards becoming a PhD student, I would like to give you a few pieces of advice that I usually give to new students in their first few days. I've hinted at some of these throughout the book, but here I shall give them explicitly. I've found over the years that those that follow this advice achieve their doctorates quickly and well.

9.1 Don't believe everything you read

Four months into my PhD, I attended my first conference. Every delegate was given a lovely book, recently published on the subject covered in the conference. During the event they had a panel discussion and on the panel was the author of the book. At the time I found this enormously exciting. I had never met a real live author before. Here was someone who had recorded their words of wisdom onto lovely glossy pages. He must be terribly clever, I thought. An author must be a special kind of expert. One that you can really trust. I looked at the guy with a real awe. And then I heard what he had to say in the panel discussion. While he clearly knew his area very well, I quickly realized that this was not Einstein. In fact, I knew a few things that he didn't. This was the beginning of my realization that books are not quite as special as they seem. Nor are journal papers or conference papers.

I'm writing a book now. There's absolutely nothing stopping me from writing something completely untrue. How about this?:

All elephants are made of cheese.

That sentence has been published in this book. Does that make it true? Clearly not. My strong advice to you as you do your research is assume everything you read is inaccurate until proven otherwise.

Researchers are not always very good at writing clearly. Sometimes they are not even very good at research. But that does not stop them from writing. It's amazing when you talk to the authors of papers or books and hear the truth. Perhaps the ground-breaking results they reported were only achieved once in five hundred experiments. Perhaps they discovered that they made a mistake in their calculations, but didn't get around to correcting the article. Perhaps it was so important for their career for them to get a research paper that they exaggerated their results by using some creative statistics. Perhaps they were not very bright and produced flawed analysis. You are going to have to read a whole lot of rubbish during your research. Part of doing your doctorate is learning to distinguish between truth and elephants made from cheese.

9.2   Keep careful records, and keep the records carefully

How many times have I heard the awful words: 'I read a hundred papers two years ago but I can't remember any of them"? Or, 'I know I did all those experiments at the start of the PhD, but it was so long ago that I've forgotten the details.' Or, 'I talked to the world expert eighteen months ago, but I forget exactly what he said.' And how many times have I heard those fateful words: 'I left my notebook on the train and I've lost everything.' Or, 'my laptop was stolen and I've lost everything.' Or, 'there was a hard disk failure and I've lost everything.' Or, 'I was transferring my work to a new computer and something went wrong and ...' You get the idea.

It's very simple. A PhD is a very long piece of research. Unless you keep excellent records, you will forget what you did and what you read. Unless you keep those records safe and backed up securely, you will surely lose them. Computers are wonderful devices, enabling you to keep detailed records, databases of everything you read, diagrams and explanations of every thought you had. It's a great idea to use one. They also enable you to make multiple back-ups of your work, which you can keep in more than one place. Most students only reach a sensible level of paranoia when they have written half their thesis and are afraid of losing it. That's the stage when they start making multiple back-ups and leaving copies with different friends and family – just in case. Your best chance of success is to be paranoid from the start and back everything up, all the time. You can either listen to this advice, or spend an extra six months at the end redoing work that you lost or forgot. Your choice.

9.3   Look after your finances – make a budget and stick to it

Over the years I've supervised rich students and poor students. Some were lucky enough to get good funding and have wealthy parents. Some paid every penny from their own savings. Without exception, by the third year they all were struggling financially, with many needing to take part-time jobs to pay their bills. Doing a doctorate is expensive and becoming more so every year. It doesn't matter how super-intelligent and creative you are, if you run out of money you will not be able to complete it. Issues like angry landlords, tuition fees and food will suddenly dominate your life.

From the very first day you should know your monthly income and outgoings. Use a notebook or a spreadsheet program and make a list. The outgoings are likely to be much more than you realize: fees, rent, food, travel, books, mobile phone, electricity, gas, water, television licence, subscription to broadband, clothes, fun. The income may be nothing more than your bursary or your loan. You must work out exactly what you can afford to spend each month, and then stick to it. If you cannot even manage your own money, you don't stand much chance of getting a doctorate.

9.4   Remember to get your admin, reports, vivas and courses done promptly

PhD supervisors rarely remember all the administration that needs to be completed for your PhD. It is normally considered your responsibility to make sure everything that needs to be done, gets done. This includes all reports written by you, all courses and examinations, all vivas[17] and even such details as whether your fees have been paid, whether you are registered as an MPhil or PhD student, whether you have officially achieved 'writing up' student status, whether the paperwork for your thesis submission and examiners has been completed and approved, and applying for funding to pay for equipment or travel.

---

[17] In many universities, a PhD will be broken up into a series of assessments with each requiring you to write a report, give a presentation and defend your work from criticism, such as a first-year viva, transfer viva, 18-month viva, yearly exhibitions, and so on.

I've known some students to become very angry with their supervisors because they were not told to complete a particular report or do a certain course. The reaction of most supervisors to this kind of behaviour is an unhelpful, 'so what?' You are the PhD student. You are considered to be bright enough to perform ground-breaking research on your own. You are also considered bright enough to check exactly what administration needs to be done and get it done, all by yourself.

You should find that your supervisor will assist you if things go wrong. But PhDs are different from undergraduate degrees and Masters courses. Every PhD is unique, and so identical procedures don't work for them. Reports are often written when you are ready to write them, so don't expect someone to tell you to do it. That doesn't mean the work is not compulsory – if you don't get the administration done, you may not be permitted to submit your thesis. Check what you need to do and make a timetable to remind yourself.

9.5 Break the work into a series of smaller projects

Almost no one can think about one thing for three years.[18] I've known several PhD students to come to me at the beginning of their doctorate and say, 'I know what I want to do, but I just don't know where to start.' I have also known PhD students who come to me at what should be the end of their doctorate and say, 'I still know what I want to do, but no matter how hard I try, I can't make any progress.'

Whether you have a grand goal or a piece of precision analysis to achieve, the human brain works best if the task is broken down into a series of smaller sub-goals. One of the most effective methods for keeping yourself motivated and making progress is to set yourself a new target every two or three months. That target should have a clear result: an article, a scientific paper, a transfer report, a piece of art, a working circuit board, a laboratory optimization, a literature review. Ideally, each result should fit into your final thesis with relatively little modification.

If you manage this trick, then you will find that you always have something to look forward to. You'll always have a target to aim for when you wake up each morning. And when you achieve the result, you can reward yourself with a short break, a nice meal, or a treat, before moving on to the next target.

There are many good reasons why this method of doing a doctorate works. First, it's a great way of managing your time and enabling you to

---

[18] Or four, for the average PhD in the UK.

achieve something big, one step at a time. Second, it gives you plenty of practice with all of the important skills you need to learn during a doctorate: writing, presenting and defending your work, meeting other researchers in the field. Third, it ensures that as much of your work gets published as possible, which means it will undergo peer review and will be more likely to satisfy your PhD examiners. Fourth, it makes writing your thesis much easier as you will have written down most of your work already. Fifth, even the process of writing helps you to understand the ideas better, so articles and papers enable you to clarify your thoughts and progress faster. Sixth (and most important), this is a way of managing your happiness – frequent achievements make you feel good; a long, hard slog towards a goal that seems infinitely far away is much more likely to be depressing.

Your supervisor can help you set your targets – perhaps suggesting relevant conferences for your article, or exhibitions for your piece. If a target turns out to be a marathon in itself, break it down into a couple of smaller steps. Just don't try to do the whole doctorate in one go. If you were sailing around the world, you would stop at many interesting places along the way – you wouldn't spend your whole time at sea.

9.6   Who's the first author?

One of the most common causes of conflict between academics (and between students and supervisors) can be authorship of papers and articles. It may seem like a very trivial point, but if you've spent two years working on a paper with no help from your supervisor and then he insists that his name appears as the first author, you may be very annoyed. In academia, multi-author papers are often cited like this: (first author et al., 2005). So if you are not the first author, your name may never appear in references made by other people. Normally the order in which authors appear is taken to indicate the level of contribution made by each author.

Most academics (and sometimes groups or departments) have a policy about authorship. On rare occasions the authors are listed alphabetically (it is usually the academics with last names beginning with 'A' who insist on this). Sometimes, because of the 'intellectual contribution' made, the supervisor will insist on having his name as the first author, or the second author, whether he's written any of the paper or not. I personally don't believe either of these approaches is fair on the student, so I have a very strict policy, which I recommend. An author should contribute to the text of a paper (hence the word 'author'). Authors should be listed in order of the actual content provided by each individual. If someone contributed intellectually but did not provide any input into the paper, they should be acknowledged in an acknowledgements section, but not listed as an author. If someone provided a small amount of content or editing, then they may be listed as a last author. So if someone wants to be an author of a paper, they must actually work on that paper, at least a little. If they can't be bothered, or can't find the time, then they should not be an author. I have refused to have my name on my students' papers when I have not had time to contribute to the text – I do not believe I should receive credit for their work.

Whatever your supervisor believes with respect to paper authorship, you should find out *before* you write a paper, and make sure you agree. If your supervisor has no strict policy, then suggest the policy above – it will give you the maximum amount of credit for your work (and encourage your supervisor to help you more).

9.7   Give credit to others when it is due

One common source of confusion for new students is how to refer to contributions to their work that have been made by other people. Such contributions will be made in many different ways: you will be reviewing the literature in your area and may well find that your work builds upon or extends the findings of others. You may also be working with other students or scientists in collaborative work, so other people may directly produce work that you use as part of your PhD research. In some circumstances you may wish to duplicate the work of others directly (for example, a figure, a chart, an equation, or a formal definition).

There are different approaches taken in other countries, but in the UK there is a very clear philosophy which you must follow. When you find that your work is related to or extends the work of someone else, you must critically review that work – summarize their work in your words, give your considered opinion of it, and *always* cite the original source and author of the material you refer to. In your thesis, you need to cite the original source for every statement you make that is derived from the work or finding of someone else. This is important, for it gives your work more credibility – you are providing a method by which your evidence can be checked and verified by others. Furthermore, if you make it seem as though the work of someone else was created by you, then you will make enemies in your own research field.

Sometimes cultural differences can make this a real problem. Over the years I have acted as organizer of many scientific conferences. On more than one occasion I have been approached by an angry scientist who complained that a paper authored by someone else in my conference contained significant amounts of text taken from his previously published paper. When I spoke to the author of the plagiarizing paper the response was always that they respected the work so much that they felt the best approach was to copy the text and figures directly into their paper.[19] The trouble was that they had not cited the author of the original material or asked permission, so it looked as though they were claiming this work was authored by them. If spotted by the reviewers, such papers are always rejected for plagiarism.

Don't do this. It's not just bad practice, it's lazy and illegal, and you will be infringing the copyright of the author and publisher. It's fine to reproduce a sentence or equation, and cite the author, for example: 'All elephants are made of cheese' (Bentley 2006).

For anything more, such as an image or large section of text, you are required to contact the copyright holder and ask permission, and also cite the author (I had to do this for some of the material in this book – see the Acknowledgements section). If you plan to reproduce images that have already been published, some publishers will require a fee to be paid. In the worst case you could be sued by the copyright holder for breach of contract.

If you have worked closely with someone else (including your supervisor) during your PhD and your thesis contains the work of others, you must clearly identify which portions were created by others and give them credit. There is nothing wrong with enlisting the help of others during your research. Just remember that you will be awarded your PhD for the work that *you* have done. Your examiners are required to check exactly what you did and did not do. There will be no way you can fool them, so don't try.

In the end, this is a very simple philosophy – you would want others to credit you for your work, so you must do the same for them. Always cite the original source, and remember that you don't need permission to summarize, criticize and cite, but you *do* need permission to duplicate.

9.8   Listen to your supervisor and, if unhappy, talk to him or to someone else

Your supervisor is your mentor, your counsellor, your confidence builder, your tutor and your guide. If you have a problem about anything, including them, you should first try to talk to them about it. A frank and open discussion will normally resolve most problems. Also remember that just because your supervisor may give you advice that you don't agree with

---

[19]   In extreme cases, entire books have been copied and republished in other countries under the name of someone else.

does not mean he's wrong or incompetent.[20] Do try to listen carefully to what your supervisor suggests. Their words are rarely random, and they are usually more likely to help than hinder.

If you feel that something is not right – perhaps you have done exactly what your supervisor has suggested for months and the expected progress has not been made – then don't be afraid of going to talk with someone else. If you have a second supervisor, talk with them. If there is a member of staff responsible for PhD students (perhaps a Research Students Coordinator), then try talking with her. If all else fails, go to the Head of Department or Dean of the School with your worries.

Like many, my own PhD followed a rough course. I began on a studentship to create a technical piece of equipment to train anaesthetists. I quickly discovered that my supervisor had an uncanny ability to get other people to do his work for him and seemed to spend extraordinary amounts of time on holiday in Egypt, meaning that I very rarely saw him. But more distressingly for me, I discovered after four months that my department could not afford the equipment I needed for my project. I voiced my concerns to my supervisor, but received what I considered to be an undue lack of concern. So I went and talked with the Dean of the School. He agreed with me that there was a serious problem, and so (much to the annoyance of my supervisor) I was allocated another supervisor and did my PhD on a different project that I suggested myself.

Not many students are so unlucky, so don't worry that you might need to find a new supervisor – such a change is quite rare. However, do remember that, like everything else in your doctorate, it will be up to you to make something happen if you're unhappy. Sitting at home worrying will not help you. Going and talking to your supervisor and others will.

9.9 Is it going to be in your thesis?

There are two occasions when I exclaim, 'Focus!' One is when I'm trying to use my old camera with the dodgy auto-focus. The other is during most

---

[20] One professor I know has a standard approach for all his students who seem to be in difficulties. He tells them to write down their thesis title, abstract and table of contents. Many of the students become frustrated at what they see as a waste of time, but what they don't realize is that when they can write a decent title, abstract and table of contents, they'll have focused their thoughts enough to be able to complete their PhDs. So this strange-sounding advice is actually a very good technique used by a highly experienced supervisor. In contrast, a better sign of incompetence is usually doing nothing. One notable example I encountered once was an academic who only attended his university for about four hours, two or three days a week. On the rare occasions that he would meet with his student, he actually fell asleep during the meetings. Add to this, his complete lack of knowledge about the subject his student was studying and you get a very unhappy student.

meetings with most of my PhD students. Learning to focus on a single topic without being distracted by all the interesting things around it is very difficult. Most students will find themselves discovering an amazing new aspect to their field (or of a completely different field) during the course of their doctorate. A high percentage of students will then feel compelled to spend weeks, months or even years pursuing this new sub-goal. When you are completely engrossed in your work, the research always feels relevant or necessary. But all too often, the student is going off on a tangent. They're spending every waking hour working on something that is quite unrelated to their main hypothesis.

The test you use to check if your work is still on track is very simple. Ask yourself whether the work will be written in your thesis. Imagine which chapter it will go into. Think about how it will form a coherent part of a single theme; how it will provide more evidence to support your central hypothesis. If you then cannot see how it fits, you have a problem. If the vast bulk of the work will end up in an appendix – why are you spending so much of your time on it?

Equally, if you have spent a huge amount of time on some research, don't be tempted to throw it away just because it didn't work out the way you wanted. Remember that research is about knowledge. Students often mistakenly believe that only their successes should be written up. In fact, the failed experiments or the disproved hypotheses often provide much more useful information than the successes. A rocket scientist needs to know what has the potential to blow him up before he needs to know how a successful rocket works. The same is true for all other areas of research – we need to know which paths lead to failure before we can find the road to success. So your ten months of work which led to the opposite result to the one you expected is a very useful contribution to knowledge. Don't throw it away.

Most PhDs are assessed purely on the basis of the thesis. You will have to do a huge amount of work before you are able to complete your thesis, but everything you do must be described in that final document, or it will contribute nothing towards your PhD. The fastest way to finish a PhD is to plan the shape of your thesis from very early on and ensure that *everything* you do has a slot in a chapter somewhere.

9.10 Insomnia happens to everyone

Insomnia is just one of many stress-related problems that most PhD students experience during their doctorate. When it happens to you (and hopefully you'll have a year or two of happiness first), just remember that you are not alone. I suffered from insomnia during my PhD, my students suffered from it, and my supervisor suffered from it during his PhD.

Stress is most common when you're obsessing about some aspect of your work and you're not giving yourself enough time off. It's made worse if you work at home because you may find it harder to get away from the work, and may keep returning to it at all hours of the day and night. My best advice to reduce this stress is to be strict with yourself. Only work between certain hours of the day. Try to go to bed and wake up at regular times. Even if there is still lots to do and you're working at home, when the time comes to stop, then you must stop for the day. You must also ensure that you get away from your work and have proper breaks. Exercise is one of the most effective ways to reduce stress – play a sport, go jogging, swimming or just take a long walk in the park. Just make sure that you exercise the body as well as your brain or you may find insomnia happens to you. Finally, never think about work before you sleep. Always make sure you have *at least* an hour of doing something different before bed.

Stress is so normal for PhD students that I advise against taking medication for the symptoms (unless your doctor recommends otherwise). Your stress will be caused by your work. To relieve the stress you need to discuss your problems with your supervisor, friends or colleagues rather than taking sleeping pills.

9.11 You are not the first person to do a PhD

We all go through difficult times during our doctorate. Sometimes it is hard to know whether what you've done is worth a doctorate. You might have convinced yourself that your work is ready for writing up in a thesis, when really it isn't. (In fact, it is much more common for students to overestimate the work required and do more than they need to, not less.) You may not be sure whether the subject that you have chosen for your PhD is good enough, or that you have read enough background papers, or that your thesis is structured properly. Perhaps you've lost trust in your supervisor and you're not entirely sure if his advice is correct. Perhaps your friends have their own worries and problems and are not listening to yours right now. The solution is simple. Your university – and probably your department – will keep copies of all of the previous PhD theses of successful students. Borrow a few of them and read them.

Once you have read a few PhD theses you soon begin to develop a feel for the style of writing that is required. You will understand the kind of subjects that were considered worthy of PhDs in the past, and you will see exactly how much work was performed by those students to get their doctorates. If you can, ask somebody in your department which theses were considered very good (you don't want to pick up tips from the bad ones). With two or three examples of good theses in front of you, you will suddenly find it possible to plan the shape of your own thesis, and see the kind of structure and content that you will have to write – and you will obtain a better idea of what you have left to do before your thesis looks like one in front of you.

You should use exactly the same trick when you need to write a paper. Find several examples of papers that were published in the same journal or conference and read them. This will help you to structure your own paper appropriately, and inform you of which topics are considered interesting and useful by that publication.

You are not the first person to do a PhD. Even if you cannot learn anything relevant from what other people did in their research, you will always be able to learn from *how* they did their research.

9.12 Communication can be fun

Even for those who are very confident about their ability to do research and achieve a PhD, there are two very common fears, particularly those for whom English is not their first language. Those fears are writing and public speaking. Both are skills that you have to perform frequently in order to improve and gain confidence. They are also skills that you can develop through experiencing how other people demonstrate them. Reading a lot will help your writing. Listening to many presentations will teach you how to present your work better.

Writing is something that you will not be able to avoid. All PhDs require you to write a substantial number of words – usually more than you will have written in one go before. Learning to write well is not something that can be taught in a book – it will take you years of practice and many, many hours with your supervisor, being told why what you have written is not good enough. Luckily, I am both a writer and a PhD supervisor, so I'll try to give a few writing tips that most students find helpful:

- Your objective is to communicate clearly, not to obscure and make yourself look clever. I could write, 'The individual traversed via pedestrianization with a destination comprising a locale dedicated to consumer–customer financial relationships' or I could write, 'The person walked to the shop.' Try to write clearly and simply: use as few words as you can, and only use terminology when absolutely necessary.
- Always try to give enough information to make your work reproducible by others. It can be more important to communicate *how* you did your work rather than the fact you did the work at all.
- Learn to read the words that you actually wrote and not what you meant to write. If I wrote 'The hare and the tortoise raced together before it won' then I might be able to read the sentence and

understand completely what I meant – but no one else in the world would understand, because it doesn't really mean anything.

- Treat your words as though they are disposable. Never spend an hour trying to perfect a sentence you're stuck on – just delete it and write it again. Your message is the important thing. You can always use new words.

- The structure and flow of a document are important. Try to plan the outline of your document first by writing headings and then filling in the details. Don't be afraid of moving chunks of text or entire sections around, if they fit better elsewhere.

- English is a very difficult language and most foreign students will make mistakes as they learn. Perhaps some of the most common errors are with the definite and indefinite articles: 'the' and 'a'. There are too many rules and exceptions to mention here, but it is sometimes useful to think of 'a' as meaning 'one example of any' and 'the' as meaning 'this/these specific'. (Unfortunately this rule does not always work, so your best solution is often to ask a native English speaker.)

The other communication skill you will need to learn is public speaking. Like many, I used to become terribly nervous at the prospect of giving a talk in front of an audience. The thought that I would one day have a job that involved speaking for an hour or more in front of hundreds of people, would have filled me with horror.

The best advice I ever had on this subject was given to me by a friend who liked ballet dancing. She simply told me to enjoy myself. They're all listening to *you*, she said, so enjoy being the centre of attention. And you know, it actually works. My approach is to be informal and give my seminars as though I'm chatting to friends. Others prefer to dress up and stand formally at a lectern. Just make sure that you are well prepared and comfortable, then go up there and have fun. If you know your mouth will get dry, take some water and have a sip at the end of a sentence or just before you change to the next slide – dramatic pauses are good. If you think your hand might get a little shaky, don't use a laser pointer – those little red dots tend to dance in time to your shakes. Make sure you've practised the whole talk a couple of times (even if it is to an empty room) so you know what you're going to say and that the talk is the right length. While it's usually not a great idea to learn lines as you'll sound stilted and over-rehearsed, knowing your opening two sentences will help you start without a hitch. If you're using slides or a computer, remember to keep the slides simple and few in number. Audiences often prefer text to equations, they prefer pictures to text, they prefer movies to pictures, and audio (music or unusual noises) to movies. You can brighten even the most technical talk with a nice image or movie – as long as they are relevant.

Remember that your objective is to communicate clearly and relevant pictures can paint a thousand words. Putting funny cartoons in your talk is not a very clever idea.

When you speak, try to talk clearly and audibly. If you need a microphone, make sure your mouth stays at the right distance from it at all times. I usually prefer a radio mike or a microphone I can hold in my hand. If the microphone is attached to the lectern, you need to remember not to speak if you turn your head to look back at your slides: the effect for the audience can be LOUD SPEECH then very quiet speech THEN LOUD SPEECH AGAIN, which is very distracting.

If English is not your first language, then it is very important that you practise speaking about your work regularly. Most universities run courses on giving talks (and other skills such as thesis and paper writing) which everyone can benefit from. But the best way to become competent at speaking in a language is to socialize with native speakers of the language. You may naturally feel more comfortable with friends who speak the same language as you, but it is important that you make friends with English-speakers and talk to them often. Your examiners will almost certainly be asking you questions in English at your viva, so you will need to be fluent and relaxed by then.

Effective public speaking requires confidence, which only comes with practice. Even if you cannot learn to enjoy it at all, every time you do it you will gain more confidence until you will no longer fear it. Remember that even the most experienced speakers get a touch of nerves before walking onto the stage. Those nerves are good – they keep you on your toes.

9.13 Enjoy yourself

Your doctorate is going to be hard work. But that does not mean that it won't be fun. If you have followed the advice in this book and found yourself a PhD place to do research that you find exciting and significant, then you are going to have a great time. Enjoy your achievements. Remember to reward yourself when you hit a target. Take advantage of everything your department has to offer – take pleasure in giving seminars to others. If you get a chance to travel to other countries for conferences, exhibitions or field trips, widen your horizons and experience the world. If your article is printed somewhere, look for your name – isn't it good to see yourself listed in that brochure, folio, proceedings or book?

There will always be tough times when you wonder why you began the whole crazy idea. But deep down you will know why you are doing this. You want that doctorate. One day you will be able to write 'Dr' in front of your name. That title will mean you have achieved something significant.

Good luck, and have a great time!

Resource guide: current funding opportunities

New PhD studentships come out every week; they are advertised in predictable places and are easy to find. Universities will have many new funded PhD places each year, detailed on their own web pages. There are also many opportunities that are provided by governments and charities that are available annually. This section describes how and where to look and what you should be applying for.

The resources are organized into seven main sections:

1   Advertised studentships
2   Small awards
3   Annual charity studentships
4   UK and EU awards
5   International awards
6   Student visa guide
7   Directory

All of these resources provide links to further information on the Internet. It is important that you check the web pages listed, to ensure you are using the most up-to-date information. If you are not familiar with computers or web-browsing, the following section provides a few hints.

Internet tricks

You will be able to do almost all of your searching using the Internet. Newspapers such as *The Times* and *Guardian* and scientific magazines such as *Nature*, *Science* and *New Scientist* are commonly used to advertise studentships, but the adverts are always placed online as well (and sometimes may appear online several days before the paper version is published).

If you have your own computer at home, remember that you may need to spend many hours searching online. Unless you have a cheap connection, you might find it sensible to connect only during off-peak times to reduce your phone bill. If you don't have a computer, all libraries in the UK have computers connected to the Internet which you will be able to use for minimal charges. The cheapest solution is of course to use your free university computers if you have access.

Once you're online, you need to run a web browser program such as Internet Explorer or Netscape. Then there are two approaches to using the Internet: type in the web address directly (and many addresses are given in this section to enable you to do exactly that) or search for the right page. A good search engine can be found at: http://www.google.com/

You'll find that if you type the words 'PhD studentship UK' into Google, you will immediately find hundreds of pages that may be of interest to you.

The frustrating thing about web pages is that the web addresses (or URLs as they are known) often change. This means that you may find some of the URLs provided in this resource section are old or out of date. Indeed, it is conceivable that some of the universities, funding mechanisms and charities may disappear or change their names, so even these lists are not infallible. However, if a URL you are trying doesn't work, all is not lost. You will often be able to make it work with a little tweaking. Here's how.

Every web address has a similar kind of format. Normally something like:

http://www.organization.ac.uk/folder/

This URL is an address that your computer uses to figure out which computer in the world to talk to, via the Internet. After the 'www', there will usually be a shortened version of the organization's name, e.g., 'ox' for Oxford or 'gla' for Glasgow University. After that you may see an '.ac.uk' which means British academic institution in the UK. If the organization is a charity, you might see a '.org' or if it is a company, you might see '.com' or '.co.uk'. The final part tells you the country, so, for example, a '.uk' means UK, a '.au' means Australian, a '.fr' means French, and a '.edu' means it's an American educational institution. After the main part of the address, you may see a slash followed by all kinds of other names and slashes. These are actually folders and file names on the remote computer.

Sometimes the main address is slightly modified. So, for example, the Computer Science Department at University College London modifies the basic UCL web address from: http://www.ucl.ac.uk/ to: http://www.cs.ucl.ac.uk/ where the 'cs' obviously refers to 'Computer Science'. (The change of address is because the Computer Science Department uses its own computers for its web pages instead of the central UCL ones.)

Once you understand how URLs work, you can very easily rewrite them slightly in your browser if the current version fails to connect. So this very long URL:

http://www.antarctica.ac.uk/About_BAS/Cambridge/Divisions/PSD/
psd_phd_vacation.html

which refers to one specific file in a very specific place on a computer
somewhere, is quite likely to fail. If it does, try just going to the root
destination: http://www.antarctica.ac.uk/ and then searching for the page
you want from there. This is likely to work because although files and
directories are changed all the time, the core addresses stay the same for
years.

When you really become comfortable with web pages, you will find that
you can navigate by rewriting addresses quite easily. For example, you may
just have the address of one word document: http://www.skill.org.uk/info/
infosheets/pg_ed.doc But might be wondering if there are any other
similar ones on the same site. You can have a look by guessing that they
may be kept here: http://www.skill.org.uk/info/

And then you may find what you are looking for. If all else fails, don't be
afraid to use Google to search for the keywords provided by each web
address in this section. So if this address is no longer valid:

http://ssl.pro-net.co.uk/home/grantreg/www/

then type 'international grants register nature' into Google and somewhere in the list of results you will see the right page.

RESOURCE 1

Advertised Studentships

In this section you will find the main web pages for listings and advertisements of current PhD studentships in the UK and elsewhere. General PhD studentship sites and sites devoted to specific research areas are provided.

The PhD studentship is one of the safest and quickest ways of obtaining funding, although competition may be fierce. Studentships are advertised usually about two months before the student should begin the research, and are available at all times of the year. Note that most have strict eligibility requirements that rule out international students. If you are interested in finding a PhD studentship, then make sure you follow these important steps:

- Check the deadline – is it still open?
- Check the area – are you qualified or experienced enough?
- Check the eligibility – are you the right nationality to receive the funding and do you have the right grades in your previous degree?
- Check the university, department, group and supervisor – are they any good?

If you're happy with what you find out, then go and see the supervisor. If you're still happy, then apply. Most students apply for several studentships before they find the right one for them – it is normal to apply for several simultaneously.

Advertised Studentships	General web pages
http://www.findaphd.com/ FindAPhD.com is a comprehensive guide to current research and PhD studentships. Their database contains details of research topics from many major universities and institutions throughout Europe.	
http://www.jobs.ac.uk/ Science, research, academic and related jobs in the UK and abroad. Subscribe to Jobs by Email for vacancies in universities, FE colleges, research institutions, commercial and public sector bodies, schools and charities.	
http://www.prospects.ac.uk/ Graduate careers and studentships website	
http://ssl.pro-net.co.uk/home/grantreg/www/ International grants register maintained by *Nature*	
http://naturejobs.nature.com/ Search for studentships advertised in *Nature*	
http://www.newscientistjobs.com/ Search for studentships advertised in *New Scientist*	
http://sciencecareers.sciencemag.org/ Search for studentships and jobs in *Science*	
http://www.jobs.thes.co.uk/ Search for studentships advertised in the UK *Times Higher Education* Supplement	
http://jobs.guardian.co.uk/ Search for studentships advertised in the UK *Guardian* newspaper	
http://www.studentmoney.org/ Searchable database of scholarships, bursaries and awards	
http://www.uksponsorship.com/ The UK Sponsorship Database – a wide range of sponsorship categories, including education	
http://fundingopps.cos.com/ COS Funding Opportunities™ claims to be the largest, most comprehensive database of available funding	
http://www.educationuk.org/ Details of current British Council scholarships	
http://www.degreeselect.com/ PhD studentships and opportunities in North America	
http://www.phds.org/ PhD studentships and opportunities in North America	
http://www.jason.edu.au/ PhD studentships and opportunities in Australia	

Resource 1 Advertised Studentships general web pages

Advertised Studentships	Specialist areas
http://www.math-jobs.com/	
Current PhDs and jobs in the area of mathematics	
http://rdfunding.org.uk/	
Extensive archive of funding and studentships for health-related research	
http://www.biomedscientistjobs.com/	
Current PhDs and jobs in the area of biomedical science	
http://www.ri.ac.uk/DFRL/postgrad_pages/studentships.htm	
PhD studentships at the Davy Faraday Research Laboratory of the Royal Institution	
http://london-research-institute.co.uk/lrijobs/jobsphd/	
PhD studentships at Cancer Research UK's London Research Institute	
http://www.britishcouncil.org.pk/scholarships/pakmeds.htm	
Scholarships for medical studies	
http://www.chemsoc.org/careers/careers.htm	
Royal Society of Chemistry jobs and studentships	
http://organicworldwide.net/jobs/	
Organic Chemistry jobs and studentships	
http://www.ifr.ac.uk/vacancies/studentships.html	
Institute of Food Research BBSRC studentships	
http://www.scholarships.ed.ac.uk/postgraduate/snh.htm	
Scottish National Heritage PhD studentships	
http://www.antarctica.ac.uk/About_BAS/Cambridge/Divisions/PSD/psd_phd_vacation.html	
Current British Antarctic Survey jobs and studentships	
http://www.nerc.ac.uk/funding/students/	
Current NERC studentships	
http://www.csl.gov.uk/aboutcsl/jobs/phd.cfm	
Details of Central Science laboratory studentships	
http://immunology.org/education/phd.htm	
Current PhDs and jobs in the area of immunology	

Resource 1   Advertised Studentships specialist areas

http://www.cfd-online.com/Jobs/listjobs.php?category=PhD%20Studentship

Current PhDs and jobs in the area of computational fluid dynamics

http://www.bmss.org.uk/vacancies.htm

Current PhDs and jobs for the British Mass Spectrometry Society

http://www.ch.cam.ac.uk/jobs/

Current jobs and studentships at Cambridge

Resource 1 Advertised Studentships
specialist areas

RESOURCE 2

Small Awards

Here you will find a few examples of smaller grants and awards available to 'top up' your finances (these are *not* suitable methods to pay your fees or living expenses). Smaller awards are normally needed to fund a visit overseas to a conference or a short collaboration. Some require your supervisor to apply on your behalf; all require you to be a registered PhD student. It is normal to need letters of recommendation from your supervisor or head of department. Many universities will have their own graduate funds that you will also be able to apply for – ask your supervisor for more details. Ideally your travel to conferences should not cost you anything – it is definitely worth your time and effort to look out for funding whenever you need to go to a conference. You will often find links to these types of grants from the web pages of research councils or funding agencies specific to your area of interest (see the directory at the back).

Small Awards	One-off conference trips and short visits

http://www.raeng.org.uk/research/researcher/travelgrant/default.htm

The Royal Academy of Engineering International Travel Grant Scheme is intended to help Engineering Researchers in the United Kingdom make study visits overseas. This enables them to remain at the forefront of new developments and be aware of corresponding activity overseas.

http://www.royalsoc.ac.uk/funding.asp?id=2348

Royal Society conference grants. Applicants in the final year of their PhD can submit an application. If successful, the award will only be given subject to the confirmation of his or her PhD at the time of the conference.

http://www.soas.ac.uk/registryfiles/scholarshipforms/tibawiapplicationform.pdf

SOAS Tibawi Trust. Dr Abdul-Latif Tibawi left a gift in his will to establish a Trust for a postgraduate award. The award is to assist postgraduate Palestinians enrolled at SOAS and may be used towards conference visits, fieldwork etc. The value of the award is £200. The closing date for receipt of application forms is January.

http://www.gbsf.org.uk/awards/e/f_butterfield.htm

The Great Britain Sasakawa Foundation Butterfield Awards for UK-Japan Collaboration in Medicine and Health aim to facilitate professional exchanges and small-scale collaborations between the UK and Japan in any relevant aspect of medicine and health.

There are no absolute restrictions on the field of research or collaboration, provided that it is one in which the UK and Japan have a mutual and beneficial interest. Among the areas likely to satisfy this criterion are, for example: genetic aspects of ageing; geriatric medicine; palliative care; diabetes; stem cell technology; child and adolescent mental health; community health care.

In principle, up to four awards of £5000 are offered annually, or a total annual commitment of £20000. Proposals for continuous funding of up to £5000 p.a. for a maximum of three years are acceptable. Applications for smaller – and, exceptionally, larger – sums can be considered, according to the project.

http://www.royalsoc.ac.uk/funding

Royal Society Science Networks.

The UK's Office of Science and Technology signed bilateral agreements with China, India, South Africa and South Korea to establish a networking scheme in each country to develop enduring partnerships between UK and overseas scientists in these countries. Under each of these agreements, both sides agreed on the need to bring together their most excellent scientists in bottom-up networking, without prior prescription of the fields of research to be covered. The aim is to establish partnerships of excellent young scientists who would then be in a position to bid for project funding through national funding structures.

Scientists in the UK wishing to undertake a networking visit to one of the countries listed above should apply directly to the Royal Society, but should ensure a copy of the application is sent to the partner organization in that country.

Scientists from other countries wishing to undertake a networking visit to the UK should contact the partner organizations in the first instance.

The two modes of networking available are:

- One-to-one meetings, typically lasting between 5 days to a maximum period of 3 months.

- Small seminars or workshops (5+5 meetings) in clearly defined topics, typically lasting up to a maximum of 4 days and with a maximum of 5 delegates from each side attending. Please note that this type of award is not intended for scientists wishing to travel to either country to attend international conferences or workshops.

Resource 2 Small Awards

RESOURCE 3

Annual Charity Studentships

Some of the charities in the UK have annual studentships to fund PhD students to perform research in their area of interest. This section provides some examples of studentships you may be able to find. Note that charities rarely support international students (unless they obtain an ORS award). Because of the nature of fundraising, the number and variety of studentships will vary from year to year. Some basic Internet searching (for 'trust', 'charity' and 'foundation' in combination with descriptors for your field) will provide many more examples applicable to specifically. Some charities require supervisors to apply for funding on your behalf. Charities mostly fund medical research; those that fund more general topics are provided first in the following list.

Resource 3 Charity Studentships

Annual Charity Studentships	Wellcome Trust

Web page: http://www.wellcome.ac.uk/node2126.html

The Wellcome Trust's Four-Year PhD Studentship Programmes are intended to provide high-quality postgraduate research training over a four-year period, culminating in the award of a PhD. The programmes are designed to permit candidates to move into an area of science for which they may not have gained the specific expertise necessary from their degree.

UK applicants should either be in the final year of their degree and expecting to obtain at least a 2:1, or already have graduated with at least a 2:1. Further inquiries, including those from non-UK applicants, should be directed to the individual programmes.

Students are recruited annually by the individual Programmes **for uptake in October** each year. Recruitment begins in the preceding December. Anyone interested in applying should contact the relevant Programme.

The scheme provides a four-year stipend, university fees at home student rates, contribution towards laboratory rotation expenses in the first year, research expenses for years 2 to 4, a contribution towards travel, a contribution towards transferable skills training.

Candidates should direct **all enquiries** to the individual programmes (go to the web page for more information).

Annual Charity Studentships	Carnegie Trust/Caledonian Research Foundation

Web page: http://www.carnegie-trust.org/our_schemes.htm

Web page: http://www.calres.co.uk/

Graduates of a Scottish university holding a degree with first-class honours in any subject and intending to pursue three years of postgraduate research for a PhD degree can be considered for the award of a Carnegie Scholarship. Applications for such scholarships, which are intended to be the premier award in Scotland, greatly outnumber the number of scholarships available. Students in their final year who are expected to achieve first-class honours may apply, withdrawing if they fail to do so. Scholarships, which can be held at any university in the United Kingdom, but usually in Scotland, provide fees, maintenance and a research and travel allowance. Scholars are also eligible to apply for Carnegie Research Grants and are sympathetically treated. Applicants, who must be nominated by a member of academic staff, must submit their applications on a form which is available online, but must be returned in hard copy, by 15 March to be considered for an award for the following session.

The Trust also administers scholarships funded by the Caledonian Research Foundation, which are held under identical conditions save that the scholarship must be held in Scotland.

Carnegie/Caledonian Scholarship Regulations

http://www.carnegie-trust.org/pdf_files/Regulations_Scholarship.pdf

and Carnegie/Caledonian Scholarship Nomination form

http://www.carnegie-trust.org/pdf_files/Application_form_scholarship.pdf

Annual Charity Studentships	Arthritis Research Campaign

Web page: http://www.arc.org.uk/research/forms/PhD/PhD.htm

A limited number of prestigious PhD studentships are awarded annually by open competition to UK university departments for projects that have clear relevance to the aims of the Arthritis Research Campaign (arc) and provide training in research in a multidisciplinary environment. Since numbers of awards are limited, geographic/numerical limitations may apply to the numbers of studentships held by a single department.

The Arthritis Research Campaign will pay a standard stipend on an increasing scale over the three-year period of the grant, the university PhD fees, and an annual contribution of £5000 towards laboratory costs.

Annual Charity Studentships	Ataxia Fund

Web page: http://www.ataxia.org.uk

Ataxia UK provides help to all people affected by ataxia, but focuses on the cerebellar ataxias. There are other organizations that can provide more help if ataxia is a part of multiple sclerosis, cerebral palsy or other conditions. One of Ataxia UK's main objectives is to fund high quality research into the ataxias. Ataxia UK aims to find causes and develop treatments to prevent the devastating effects of the ataxias.

Ataxia UK has been funding a range of projects over the years, from basic science research (such as understanding the disease mechanism of a particular ataxia) to more applied research including pilot trials of therapeutic interventions.

Ataxia UK has launched a new PhD studentship fund to encourage new promising scientists to start a career in ataxia research. Further information is available by email from research@ataxia.org.uk

Annual Charity Studentships	British Heart Foundation

Web page: http://www.bhf.org.uk/ (search for PhD studentships)

The British Heart Foundation provides three types of PhD studentship:

1 Established investigators may apply for a named or unnamed PhD studentship to enable a graduate to proceed to a PhD degree at a university in the UK. As a minimum requirement, the candidate must obtain an upper second-class honours degree. Awards are for three years and applicants may apply for funds to cover stipend (at BHF rates), university fees and up to £7000 a year for research consumables, which must be fully justified. Routine laboratory equipment and consumables will not be covered.

2 Clinical PhD studentships are for medically qualified candidates wishing to undertake a PhD degree over three years at a university in the UK. The candidate must be named and medically registered prior to making the application. Evidence must be submitted to show that registration for a PhD degree would be accepted by the university. The award covers salary at the appropriate point of the NHS (or clinical academic equivalent) scale and research consumables up to £7000 a year which must be fully justified. University fees, routine laboratory equipment and consumables will not be covered.

Resource 3   Charity Studentships

3 MBPhd studentships are open to UK institutions which participate in MBPhD programmes, for named candidates only who hold a first-or upper second-class honours degree. Candidates will have undertaken their pre-clinical training in the UK and have completed an intercalated BSc. The awards are for between two and three years (in accordance with the institution's scheme rules) during the candidate's MBBS training. The award covers a stipend (at BHF rates), university fees and up to £7000 a year for research consumables which must be fully justified. Routine laboratory equipment and consumables will not be covered.

Annual Charity Studentships	Cancer Research UK

Web page: http://science.cancerresearchuk.org/gapp/grantapplications/tcdb/tcd_phd?version=2#students

Cancer Research UK funds a PhD studentship scheme at its institutes and across the UK to support the training of graduate students leading to the presentation of a PhD.

The duration of the studentship will be four years and a generous stipend, standard university consolidated fees for postgraduate students (and college fees at the Universities of Oxford or Cambridge) and running expenses are provided. The fourth year of funding will provide 12 months of stipend and fees but only 6 months of laboratory running expenses, as students are expected to be winding up their laboratory work and concentrating on writing up during the final six months. All students are expected to submit their thesis by the end of the fourth year.

This scheme is run as an annual competition. Applications are advertised in *Nature* and *New Scientist* in October/November. Funding will be available from the following October. Candidates are advised to apply early as most interviews are held in January/February.

Annual Charity Studentships	Leukaemia Research Fund

Web page: http://www.lrf.org.uk/

The Gordon Piller PhD Studentships Scheme is a prestigious, competitive PhD scheme that has been designed to attract and retain some of our best science graduates in leukaemia research. Up to four studentships will be approved for funding each year.

Each award carries a stipend of £14,850 (London) or £12,730 (outside London) per annum plus fees together with an allowance of £10,600 towards research costs.

The Fund releases details of the studentship in the January edition of *Nature* journal. Closing date for applications is late February. Applicants need to apply to the relevant supervisor detailed in the studentship advertisements enclosing their full curriculum vitae together with the names and addresses of two academic referees. Applicants should hold, or expect to obtain a first-or upper second-class honours degree or equivalent in a suitable subject.

Tel 020 7405 0101 for further details.

Annual Charity Studentships	Migraine Trust

Web page: http://www.migrainetrust.org/research/grants.shtml

The Migraine Trust funds basic and clinical research into the causes of migraine, and into ways of treating, managing, and curing the condition. The Trust invites applications from researchers based at hospitals and universities on a world-wide basis, endeavouring to support the best research wherever it is taking place. The Trust also recognizes that training researchers, and encouraging researchers into this field, is vital to the future of migraine research. They therefore provide funding for both PhD studentships and training fellowships. Application forms for grants for PhD studentships within the headache field can be obtained from:

The Migraine Trust, 55–56 Russell Square, London WC1B 4HP.

Telephone: 020 7436 1336, Fax: 020 7436 2880

These should be submitted with five copies no later than 31 December.

Annual Charity Studentships	Pathological Society

Web page: http://www.pathsoc.org.uk/pathCda/cda/microSupportPhd.do?vid=2

In 1995, the Pathological Society of Great Britain and Ireland established a PhD sponsorship scheme. Applications are invited from members of the society in good standing for at least 12 months who wish to act as supervisors of a project which will lead to the award of a PhD for the student carrying out the work under their supervision.

Support will be given for a three-year PhD studentship and will cover stipend, tuition fees (UK only), a research training and support grant and a conference allowance (at Medical Research Council levels, with London Weighting if applicable). Payments will be made in three annual instalments, normally in September.

The availability of such PhD sponsored studentships will be announced through scheduled mailings to members of the Society. The closing date for applications for the commencement of a project is 1 February in the year the project is schedule to begin.

Please note: The Pathological Society is a registered charity which is not in a position to provide full economic costs or overheads with regard to any funds awarded.

Annual Charity Studentships	Royal Society of Edinburgh

Web page: http://www.royalsoced.org.uk/research_fellowships/lloydstsb.htm

The Lloyds TSB Fellowships and Studentships are advertised late in the year for awards to be taken up in October the following year.

Under the title, 'The Ageing Population', fellowships and scholarships can cover all aspects of the ageing process, for example, the medical, psychological, sociological and economic consequences of old age and the research proposed must aim at improving the quality of life.

Resource 3 Charity Studentships

Personal Research Fellowships are tenable for up to three years and are for post-doctoral research. Support Research Fellowships are for existing members of academic staff who have held their appointments for at least five years. They are normally tenable for one year and provide funding for a replacement, to enable the Fellow to take study leave whilst remaining in continuous employment with present employer.

Studentships are tenable for three years and are for graduates with first-class or upper second-class degrees for independent research leading to doctorate or equivalent qualification.

Contact the Research Awards Co-ordinator <resfells@royalsoced.org.uk>

Resource 3 Charity Studentships

RESOURCE 4

UK and EU Awards	

If you are an EU or UK citizen, then you will be eligible for funding from the UK Research Councils. Many university departments will be allocated a few studentships each year, to be used at the discretion of the department to fund the best PhD applicants. These are sometimes advertised on departmental web pages (although not always). Competition for these funded places is usually very high – unless you are a genius with stunning exam grades, it is essential for you to meet your potential supervisor and get them to back your application for any real chance of success.

If an academic has successfully been awarded a research grant, then this may generate a PhD studentship which will be advertised in the guides given in the first resource. Likewise, if a company has successfully been awarded a CASE studentship, this will also be advertised in the same places. More details of how to apply for CASE awards, together with a list of industrial CASE company and agent contacts, can be found on the EPSRC website:

http://www.epsrc.ac.uk/PostgraduateTraining/IndustrialCASE/

The other main types of funded doctorate for UK and EU citizens are the Engineering Doctorate and New Route PhD™. The EngD is a four-year scheme run in collaboration with a company. There are now many Engineering Doctorate Centres in the UK, which all have several funded places each year. This resource lists the different centres and their areas of research. At the time of writing, competition for EngDs was much less than for ordinary PhDs, making your chances of success considerably higher. Once again, it is important to meet your potential EngD supervisor, and sensible to meet the director of the EngD scheme who will be able to tell you about the courses and requirements for their EngD.

The New Route PhD™ is a similar concept to the EngD – it is even newer and also comprises a four-year scheme with taught element. At the time of writing there were 34 participating universities which offer this form of doctorate, many offering scholarships. Some of these also support Split PhDs, where you register with the participating university but undertake some or all of your research at a different university (possibly in your home country). This resource lists all the participating universities, the subject areas supported and whether they allow Split PhDs.

Because EngDs and New Route PhDs™ have a taught component, they often require students to begin at the start of the academic year (late September or October). If you are interested in doing these forms of doctorate, you should make enquiries at the centre at least six months before the start. New EngD centres and participating universities for New Route PhDs™ are appearing all the time, so remember to do your own web search to obtain a more up-to-date idea of your options.

UK and EU Awards	Engineering Doctorate (EngD) Centres

EngD in Engineering Metals for High Performance Applications in Aerospace and Related Technologies

Location: Birmingham University

Subject: Engineering Metals for High Performance Applications in Aerospace and Related Technologies

Web link: http://www.eng.bham.ac.uk/metallurgy/pg/engd/htm

EngD in Formulation Engineering

Location: Birmingham University

Subject: Formulation Engineering, microscale structure of formulated products to the macroscale processing

Web link: http://www.eng.bham.ac.uk/chemical/pg/engd/index.htm

Enhanced Engineering Doctorate Programme

Location: Cranfield University

Subject: Aerospace, Manufacturing Systems Engineering, Advanced Computational Engineering, Water Science and Environmental Engineering

Web link: http://www.ccoa.aero/courses/engd.asp

EngD in Photonics Engineering

Location: Heriot-Watt/Strathclyde/St Andrews Universities

Subject: All aspects of Photonics, including telecommunications, high power laser materials processing and optical sensing

Web link: http://www.photonics-engd.hw.ac.uk

EngD in Nondestructive Evaluation

Location: Imperial College London

Subject: Nondestructive Evaluation

Web link: http://www.rcnde.ac.uk

EngD in Electronic System Level Design

Location: Institute for System Level Integration – Edinburgh/Glasgow/Heriot Watt Universities

Subject: Electronic System Level Design, System-on-Chip Technology

Web link: http://www.sli-institute.ac.uk/student/engd/home.htm

Centre for Innovative and Collaborative Engineering

Location: Loughborough University

Subject: Construction Engineering, General Engineering

Web link: http://www.lboro.ac.uk/cice

EngD in Power Electronics, Drivers and Machines

Location: Newcastle University

Subject: Power Electronics, Drivers and Machines

Web link: http://www.ncl.ac.uk/eece/research/groups/drives/engdoc.htm

EngD in Transport Knowledge and Systems Engineering

Location: Southampton University

Subject: Transport Knowledge and Systems Engineering

Web link: http://www.soton.ac.uk/geotech/EngD/index.htm

EngD in Environmental Technology

Location: Surrey/Brunel Universities

Subject: Environmental Technologies

Web link: http://www.surrey.ac.uk/eng/pg/ces/engd/index.htm

EngD in Manufacture: Process and Product Engineering

Location: University of Manchester

Subject: Engineering for Manufacture: Process and Product Engineering

Web link: http://www.gssem.man.ac.uk/regulations/07engd.htm

Engineering Doctorate Centre in Communications

Location: University College London

Subject: Systems, Network to Services, Applications

Web link: http://www.ee.ucl.ac.uk/engd/

EngD in Bioprocess Leadership

Location: University College London

Subject: The Bioprocess Leadership Programme

Web link: http://www.ucl.ac.uk/biochemeng/department/PG_programmes.html#7

EngD in Virtual Environments, Imaging and Visualisation

Location: University College London

Subject: Virtual Environments, Imaging and Visualisation

Web link: http://www.ee.ucl.ac.uk/engd/what.html

EngD in Environmental Engineering Science

Location: University College London

Subject: Environmental Engineering Science

Web link: http://www.civeng.ucl.ac.uk/EngD/

EngD in Molecular Modelling and Materials Simulation

Location: University College London

Subject: Post-Graduate Degree in Molecular Modelling and Materials Simulation

Web link: http:www.chem.ucl.ac.uk/research/postgraduate/engdadvert.html

EngD in Steel Technology

Location: University of Wales Swansea

Subject: Steel Technology

Web link: http://www.swansea.ac.uk/engd

EngD in Manufacturing Systems Engineering

Location: Warwick University

Subject: Manufacturing Systems Engineering

Web link: http://www.warwick.ac.uk/engd/

UK and EU Awards	New Route PhD™ Participating Universities

General information: http://www.newroutephd.ac.uk/

1 University of Bath

Subjects covered by scheme: Biological sciences / Mathematical sciences / Physical sciences

2 University of Birmingham

Subjects covered by scheme: Education / Engineering and technology / Humanities / Medicine and dentistry / Physical sciences / Social, economic and political studies

3 University of Bradford

Subjects covered by scheme: Biological sciences / Computer science / Physical sciences / Social, economic and political studies

(support for Split PhD)

4 University of Brighton

Subjects covered by scheme: Biological sciences / Computer science / Creative arts and design / Social, economic and political studies

(support for Split PhD)

5 Brunel University

Subjects covered by scheme: Biological sciences / Business and administrative studies / Computer science / Education / Engineering and technology / Humanities / Mathematical sciences / Social, economic and political studies

6 Cardiff University

Subjects covered by scheme: Architecture, building and planning / Education / Social, economic and political studies

(support for Split PhD)

7 Cranfield University

Subjects covered by scheme: Engineering and technology (Manufacturing / Marine Technology / Land and Water Management / Water Sciences)

8 University of Durham

Subjects covered by scheme: tba

9 University of East Anglia

Subjects covered by scheme: Humanities / Languages / Physical sciences

10 University of Essex

Subjects covered by scheme: Computer science / Social, economic and political studies

11 University of Exeter

Subjects covered by scheme: Education / Humanities / Social, economic and political studies

12 Heriot-Watt University

Subjects covered by scheme: Mathematical sciences / Physical sciences

13 University of Hull

Subjects covered by scheme: Business and administrative studies / Engineering and technology / Humanities / Physical sciences / Social, economic and political studies

14 Imperial College of Science, Technology and Medicine

Subjects covered by scheme: Agriculture and related subjects / Biological sciences / Physical sciences / Social, economic and political studies

(support for Split PhD)

15 Keele University

Subjects covered by scheme: Social, economic and political studies

16 University of Kent at Canterbury

Subjects covered by scheme: Business and administrative studies / Social, economic and political studies

(support for Split PhD)

17 King's College London

Subjects covered by scheme: Social, economic and political studies

(support for Split PhD)

18 Lancaster University

Subjects covered by scheme: Business and administrative studies / Mathematical sciences / Physical sciences / Social, economic and political studies

19 University of Leeds

Subjects covered by scheme: Biological sciences / Computer science / Education

20 University of Leicester

Subjects covered by scheme: Engineering and technology / Humanities / Physical sciences / Social, economic and political studies / Subjects allied to medicine

(support for Split PhD)

21 Loughborough University

Subjects covered by scheme: Business and administrative studies / Engineering and technology / Librarianship and information science / Social, economic and political studies

22 University of Manchester

Subjects covered by scheme: Biological sciences / Education / Humanities / Physical sciences / Social, economic and political studies

(support for Split PhD)

23 University of Manchester Institute of Science and Technology (UMIST)

Subjects covered by scheme: Engineering and technology / Physical sciences

(support for Split PhD)

24 University of Newcastle upon Tyne

Subjects covered by scheme: Architecture, building and planning / Biological sciences / Education / Engineering and technology / Humanities / Languages

(support for Split PhD)

25 University of Nottingham

Subjects covered by scheme: Agriculture and related subjects / Architecture, building and planning / Biological sciences / Computer science / Education / Engineering and technology / Humanities / Languages / Law / Medicine and dentistry / Physical sciences / Social, economic and political studies / Subjects allied to medicine

(support for Split PhD)

26 University of Plymouth

Subjects covered by scheme: Biological sciences / Physical sciences

27 University of Portsmouth

Subjects covered by scheme: Business and administrative studies / Social, economic and political studies

(support for Split PhD)

28 University of Reading

Subjects covered by scheme: Biological sciences / Social, economic and political studies

(support for Split PhD)

29 University of Sheffield

Subjects covered by scheme: Architecture, building and planning / Business and administrative studies / Computer science / Education / Engineering and technology / Mathematical sciences / Medicine and dentistry / Social, economic and political studies

30 University of Southampton

Subjects covered by scheme: Computer science / Engineering and technology / Physical sciences / Social, economic and political studies

(support for Split PhD)

31 University of Sunderland

Subjects covered by scheme: Computer science / Creative arts and design / Subjects allied to medicine

(support for Split PhD)

32 University of Sussex

Subjects covered by scheme: Business and administrative studies / Education / Law / Social, economic and political studies

33 University of Warwick

Subjects covered by scheme: tba

(support for Split PhD)

34 University of the West of England Bristol

Subjects covered by scheme: Creative arts and design / Humanities

(support for Split PhD)

Resource 4 UK and EU Awards
New Route PhDs™

RESOURCE 5

International Awards

If you are an international student (you are not from the UK or from an EU country), then you will be expected to pay international fees – often four or five times that of 'home fees'. This is often enough to prevent many students from ever beginning their doctorates in the UK. However, there are many international awards designed expressly for students such as you. Some, like the ORSAS, only contribute some of the costs and may be used in combination with other awards. Others are designed to pay the entire costs. This section lists some of the major awards available and provides some examples of more specific awards that different institutes may maintain themselves. It also provides an example of a successful ORSAS form to help you prepare your own.

International awards can be complicated and time-consuming to apply for. They all have highly detailed eligibility requirements that you must carefully check before applying. Some require your supervisor, department, university or embassy to apply on your behalf. Most must be completed many months before your proposed PhD start date – some have deadlines a year in advance.

Luckily there are now many ways to receive assistance. Many of the larger awards provide their own help for you on their web sites. While your supervisor may not know all the details, there should be finance staff in the department or university who can help. If not, there are many general web sites designed to help you (see the directory in the final section).

Resource 5 International Awards

International Awards	Overseas Research Students Awards Scheme

Web page: http://www.universitiesuk.ac.uk/ors/

The Overseas Research Students Awards Scheme (ORSAS) was set up by the Secretary of State for Education and Science in 1979 to attract high-quality international students to the United Kingdom to undertake research. The Scheme is administered by Universities UK on behalf of the Department for Education and Skills (DfES) and is funded through the four UK higher education funding bodies (for England, Scotland, Wales and Northern Ireland).

The awards provide funding to pay the difference between the international student tuition fees and the home/EU student tuition fees charged by the academic institution that the student attends/will be attending. ORSAS awards do not cover the home/EU fee element, maintenance or travel expenses. New awards are granted annually, on a competitive basis, to international postgraduate students of outstanding academic ability and research potential. The number of new awards made each year is subject to the funding available but they are generally able to grant around 800–850. The only two criteria for winning an award are: (1) academic ability; and (2) research potential.

To be eligible you must be an international (non-EU) student who has been accepted (conditionally or unconditionally) for admission by a participating UK institution as a full-time, postgraduate research student for the next academic session; or international (non-EU) student who is registered at a participating UK institution as a full-time, postgraduate research student at the time of application.

The level of competition for ORSAS scholarships is very high and only those students who, by the time they take up their award, hold an undergraduate degree with either first-class or very good upper-second class honours (or the equivalent) will be considered. There are no restrictions on the research subject area. ORSAS awards are valid for arts/humanities and science-based subjects.

To qualify for the award, students must register at the institution concerned by 31 July. Awards are valid only from the date of registration and any student unable to register by the stipulated date will forfeit his or her entitlement to the award.

ORSAS awards cannot be held concurrently with fully-funded scholarships such as a Dorothy Hodgkin Postgraduate Award, a Marshall Scholarship or one held under the Commonwealth Scholarship and Fellowship Plan. Apart from these restrictions, other scholarships/awards may be held concurrently with an ORSAS award providing they do not cover the same area of funding (i.e. the difference between international and home/EU fees).

Payment of ORSAS awards is made directly to the institution; no money will be paid to the student. Awardholders should produce the official ORSAS award offer letter when registering at their institution, as proof of his/her award.

ORSAS awards are granted for one year in the first instance but will be renewed, subject to the awardholder's satisfactory progress, for a second and/or third year – up to a maximum tenure of nine terms or three years, providing the awardholder is still engaged in full-time research. Awardholders are not required to apply for renewal of their award; the institution will do so on their behalf providing he or she is making satisfactory progress.

Resource 5   International Awards

Application packs (in hard copy and electronic format) will be available from all participating UK higher education institutions. Application packs will not be supplied to candidates by the ORSAS office. Candidates should obtain their application packs from the institution where they have been offered a place to study for a full-time, postgraduate research degree. The ORSAS Administrator at the institution should be contacted in the first instance.

As the number of awards offered each year is strictly limited by the funding available, each participating institution is allocated a quota which represents the maximum number of applications it may submit in the annual competition. After receiving the completed applications, institutions will carry out an initial internal selection process in which they will choose those applications they deem most likely to succeed in the competition. This is why candidates are asked to submit their applications to their institutions in the first instance. Only those applications chosen by the institution will be forwarded to the ORSAS Committee for inclusion in the competition. Institutions will inform candidates at this stage whether or not their application has been forwarded to the ORSAS Committee. The results of the competition will be announced in early May.

The next four pages provide an example of a real ORSAS application form which successfully received funding. It is not a difficult form to complete; the two important aspects are good academic qualifications and a good research proposal. You should enlist the help of your potential supervisor to produce a concise proposal. Thanks to Udi Schlessinger for his permission to reproduce his form.

Resource 5 International Awards

ORS/1

ORSAS
Overseas Research Students
Awards Scheme

Application for an Award for Session 2005-2006

Boxes for completion by Academic Institution

Student's surname and initials	Subject	HESA code	HEI no	Student no
			2005	

Before completing this form, please ensure you have read the accompanying OR SAS booklet OR S/4 entitled 'Guidelines for Students'. Please complete this form in typescript or handwrite/print it clearly in black ink. The completed form should be returned to the academic institution at which you intend to study for your postgraduate research degree.
DO NOT SUBMIT YOUR APPLICATION DIRECTLY TO THE ORSAS OFFICE.

1. Academic Institution
   through which Application is made
   (See para 3.1 of Guidelines for Students)

   UNIVERSITY COLLEGE LONDON

2. Personal details

   Surname or family name   SCHLESSINGER   (IN BLOCK CAPITALS)

   Other names in full   EHUD

   Full postal address at which
   you can be contacted
   from 1 May 2005.

   This is the address to which
   your letter advising you whether
   you have been successful will
   be posted.

   GOWER STREET

   LONDON

   WC1E 6BT

   E-mail   udiemail@address.com

3. Were you already studying in the United Kingdom when you made this application?   Yes ☐   No X   Please tick appropriate box

---

Certificate to be signed by the Registrar/Secretary/ORSAS Administrator of the Academic Institution

(i)   I certify that to the best of my knowledge the academic qualifications of the applicant are as shown on page 2.

(ii) I confirm that the applicant has been accepted for admission as a registered research student and has been assigned
      appropriate supervision for a full-time course of study, commencing in Session 2005-2006, for the postgraduate
      degree of   in the Faculty/School of
      subject to the following conditions:

      Or I confirm that the applicant is registered as a research student, has been assigned appropriate supervision and is
      undertaking a full-time course of study for the postgraduate degree of
      in the Faculty/School of
      The student started the course on:

(iii) I certify that the application is made with the approval and support of this academic institution, on whose behalf
      I accept the conditions set out in OR SAS booklet OR S/5 'Guidelines for Institutions'.

(iv) Should this applicant be successful in obtaining an OR SAS award, the amount of the award receivable by this
      institution for 2005-06 academic session would be £   This amount reflects the appropriate
      flat-fee rate for the type of research activity to be undertaken which is: (1) classroom based (2) laboratory based
      (3) clinical. The institution is: (1) outside London (2) in inner London (3) in outer London. [Please delete accordingly.]

(v)   The institution's standard fee for international students for this research activity is £
      and the home students rate is £

Official Stamp of the
Academic Institution

Signed
Position
Date

4.   Research course proposed

(a)   Topic or field of research proposed

> COMPUTER SCIENCE / NEUROSCIENCE

(b)   Type of postgraduate degree for which you have been (conditionally) accepted for full-time study (e.g. PhD, MPhil)

> PHD

(c)   Department, School or Faculty to which you have applied

> INSTITUTE OF OPHTHALMOLOGY,
> FACULTY OF BIOMEDICAL SCIENCES

(d)   Start date

> SEPTEMBER 2003

If you have been accepted conditionally, please state the conditions you have to fulfil for unconditional acceptance

(e)   Give a brief description (not exceeding 150 words) of your proposed research project:

> LIGHT STIMULI ARE AMBIGUOUS WITH RESPECT TO THEIR BEHAVIOURAL SIGNIFICANCE, SINCE THEY CONFLATE MULTIPLE ASPECTS OF THE NATURAL WORLD. ANY STIMULUS CAN THEREFORE SIGNIFY AN INFINITE NUMBER OF POSSIBLE SOURCES, EACH REQUIRING A DIFFERENT RESPONSE FOR SURVIVAL. CLEARLY, NATURAL SYSTEMS RESOLVE STIMULUS AMBIGUITY; HOW EXACTLY REMAINS A FUNDAMENTAL QUESTION OF NEUROSCIENCE AND MACHINE VISION RESEARCH. DURING MY PHD, I WILL TEST THE HYPOTHESIS THAT AN UNDERSTANDING OF VISION RESIDES IN CORRELATING THE FUNCTIONAL STRUCTURE OF VISION WITH THE STATISTICS OF STIMULI AND THEIR ECOLOGICAL, HISTORICAL SIGNIFICANCE. MY RESEARCH AIM IS TO EVOLVE NEURAL NETWORKS WITHIN ECOLOGICALLY RELEVANT VIRTUAL ENVIRONMENTS IN WHICH THE AGENTS' ARCHITECTURE, THE STATISTICS OF THE IMAGES THEY EXPERIENCE, AND THE BEHAVIOURAL SIGNIFICANCE OF THOSE STATISTICS ARE KNOWN AND MANIPULATED; THUS, ENABLING THE ELUCIDATION OF THE COMPUTATIONAL PRINCIPLES OF VISION. IN PURSUING THIS PROJECT, I SHALL ESTABLISH EXPERTISE IN MANY FIELDS INCLUDING EVOLUTIONARY COMPUTATION, COMPLEXITY THEORY, VISUAL SCIENCE.

Resource 5 International Awards
ORSAS

5.   Previous higher education

(a)   Degrees or other qualifications held. Please attach a transcript of your student record if available – see paras 4.9 and 4.10 of Guidelines for Students).

(a)   Degrees or other qualifications held

University or College	Subject(s) studied	No. of years studied	Type of degree	Class/grade of degree	Dates
NEW YORK UNIVERSITY	COMPUTER SCIENCE	2 YEARS	MSC	3.92 / 4.00	MAY 2000
THE HEBREW UNIVERSITY OF JERUSALEM	ECONOMICS AND BUSINESS ADMINISTRATION	3 YEARS	BA	88.5 / 100	SEPT 1997

(b)   Qualifications for which you are currently studying

University or College	Subject(s) studied	No. of years studied to date	Type of degree	Date of final examination

6.   Professional or other qualifications (where and when did you obtain them)

7.   Particulars and date of any full-time employment (including any industrial experience or training)
(a)   In United Kingdom

(b)   Outside the United Kingdom

11/2002 – PRESENT : SYSTEMS PROGRAMMER   YALE UNIVERSITY, SCHOOL OF MEDICINE, NEW HAVEN, CT, USA
04/2001 – 11/2002 : LEAD JAVA PROGRAMMER / PROJECT LEADER   INFO-X, NORTHVALE, NJ, USA
07/1997 – 06/1998 : SOFTWARE DEVELOPER   XPERT OFFICE NETWORKS, BNEI BRAK, ISRAEL

8. Other relevant information (please include details of any publications)

9. Where did you learn about the Overseas Research Students Awards Scheme?

I HEARD ABOUT IT FROM LAURA SHORT, THE SCHOLARSHIPS ADVISOR AT THE INSTITUTE OF OPHTHALMOLOGY

10. References (Only two references may be submitted)

Give names, titles and full addresses of TWO referees who are most familiar with your academic work and are prepared to write about your academic ability and research potential. The first referee should be a teacher who has direct knowledge of your first/undergraduate degree work OR a referee with knowledge of your postgraduate studies if a first degree referee is difficult to locate. The second referee should be the supervisor/head or senior member of the department, school or faculty where you will be undertaking your research. The referees will be contacted by the academic institution concerned.

First Referee

Name   PROF MSC SUPERVISOR

Address   COMPUTER SCIENCE DEPT

NEW YORK UNIVERSITY

MERCER ST, NEW YORK

NY 10012, USA

Email   emailaddress@cs.nyu.edu

Position   PROFESSOR

Second Referee

Name   PROF AT OPHTHALMOLOGY

Address   INSTITUTE OF OPHTHALMOLOGY

UNIVERSITY COLLEGE LONDON

BATH STREET, LONDON EC1V 9EL

Email   emailaddress@ucl.ac.uk

Position   PROFESSOR

11. Signature of applicant

I sign below to confirm that I have read, understood and agree to comply with the ORSAS regulations and conditions of offer as set out in the ORSAS booklet ORS/4 entitled 'Guidelines for Students'. I UNDERSTAND THAT I WILL BE DISQUALIFIED FROM THE COMPETITION IF I HAVE APPLIED FOR AN ORSAS AWARD THROUGH MORE THAN ONE INSTITUTION IN THIS 2005-06 COMPETITION.

Please note that unsigned, undated applications will not be accepted.

Signature   Ehud Schlessinger   Date   3 May 2003

Resource 5 International Awards
ORSAS

International Awards	Dorothy Hodgkin Postgraduate Award Scheme

Web page: http://www.rcuk.ac.uk/hodgkin/

In November 2003 the Prime Minister launched the Dorothy Hodgkin Postgraduate Award Scheme (DHPA). The scheme is a new UK initiative to bring outstanding students from India, China, Hong Kong, South Africa, Brazil, Russia and the developing world to come and study for PhDs in top-rated UK research facilities. The pilot in 2004 funded 129 PhD students, with 160 funded the following year.

The scheme is open to top quality science, engineering, medicine, social science and technology students from overseas to study for PhDs over a period of three to four years, at an average annual cost per student of £25,000 (each DHPA is valued at £75,000) primarily to cover fees and maintenance. The overriding criterion of the scheme is excellence, and DHPA scholars should be easily recognizable as the 'best of the best'.

Each scholarship is jointly funded by one public sector (Research Council) and one private sector partner, and will be badged to show this relationship (for example a Vodafone-EPSRC Dorothy Hodgkin Postgraduate Award). For each scholarship, the area of study to be undertaken must be within the remit of the associated Research Council. It is also a requirement of the scheme that DHPA scholars are placed in departments RAE-rated 5 or higher (or in a Research Council Research Institute considered to be of equivalent quality).

The scheme is open only to student nationals from India, China, Hong Kong, South Africa, Brazil, Russia and the developing world, as defined by the Development Assistance Committee of the OECD. The Office of Science and Technology publishes a full list of eligible countries.

Recipient universities are required to ensure that the students they accept hold a high-grade qualification, at least the equivalent of a UK first-class honours degree, from a prestigious academic institution. These students should be considered to be the 'best of the best' (for example, candidates should be demonstrably in the top 20 per cent of PhD candidates). Students must be selected in accordance with the university's own postgraduate admission requirements. Universities participating in the scheme will be required to apply the Foreign and Commonwealth Office Voluntary Vetting Scheme to successful scholarship applications.

Recipient universities are listed here:

http://www.rcuk.ac.uk/hodgkin/uni_list.asp

Frequently asked questions for students:

http://www.rcuk.ac.uk/hodgkin/faqs_students.asp

Point of contacts:

http://www.rcuk.ac.uk/hodgkin/uni_contacts.asp

Resource 5 International Awards

International Awards	British Chevening Scholarships

Web site: http://www.chevening.com/

The Chevening Scholarship Programme is a truly global programme and operates in over 150 countries around the world. As the programme is so diverse and far-reaching there is not a single timetable for applications and so it is important that you check with the local office when the deadline for applications in your country is. Although the timetable for deadlines may change from country to country, the application process remains the same. Each country will advertise when they are inviting applications for Chevening scholarships and will state their deadline for applications. If you are eligible and shortlisted, you will be interviewed by a panel consisting of a member of the British Embassy and the British Council.

There are three types of scholarship:

Type A scholarships – which cover tuition fees only.

Type B scholarships – full scholarships that cover tuition fees, monthly stipend and various one-off allowances.

Type C scholarships – these vary from award to award and cover part/full stipend and/or allowances.

Competition for Chevening scholarships is intense, and only one in every 25 applicants is successful. A typical successful applicant would be:

- A graduate with proven academic skills.

- Committed to return to their country and contribute to the socio-economic development of their country through implementing the new skills and knowledge acquired in the UK.

- Established in a career, with a track record of excellence and achievement, and the prospect of becoming a leader in his/her chosen field. The vast majority of Chevening scholars are aged 25–35 years old.

- Be able to show at interview that they possess the personal qualities to benefit from their scholarship and use it to succeed in their chosen career.

- Have a clear idea how their scholarship will benefit their country on their return.

- Have good English Language skills, as most UK higher education institutions require a minimum IELTS of 6.5 for admission on to postgraduate courses.

PhD funding is normally only considered when there is a co-funding partner who will provide some of the necessary funds.

Resource 5 International Awards

International Awards	Commonwealth Scholarships & Fellowships Plan

Web sites, http://www.acu.ac.uk/cusac/

http://www.csfp-online.org/hostcountries/uk/

Commonwealth Scholarships & Fellowships Plan (CSFP) awards in the United Kingdom are administered by the Commonwealth Scholarship Commission, a non-Departmental Public Body established by Parliament. Government funding for awards comes from the Department for International Development, which supports awards for developing Commonwealth countries, and the Foreign and Commonwealth Office, which supports awards for other Commonwealth countries. The Commission Secretariat is provided by the Association of Commonwealth Universities, based in London. Financial provision, welfare and other support are provided by the British Council.

Commonwealth countries under this scheme are: Australia, Botswana, Brunei Darussalam, Cameroon, Canada, Ghana, India, Jamaica, Malaysia, Malta, Mauritius, New Zealand, Nigeria, South Africa, Trinidad and Tobago, United Kingdom.

Two types of scholarships are supported:

1 General scholarships

General scholarships are open to Commonwealth citizens and British-protected persons permanently resident in any Commonwealth country other than the United Kingdom. The majority of awards are tenable at any approved institution of higher education in the United Kingdom. In recent years, however, a minority of awards have been funded jointly with specific universities. Awards are available for the duration of the course of study or research degree concerned, up to a maximum of 36 months. General Scholarships represent the largest scheme offered by the Commission, with 120–150 awards made annually.

The scholarships cover university fees, scholar's return travel, book allowance, apparatus, approved study travel, personal maintenance (plus allowances, where applicable, for spouses and children). Nominations from agencies must be received in London by 31 December in the year preceding the award being taken up. Applications must be made in the first instance to the Commonwealth Scholarship agency in the country in which the applicant has his or her permanent home.

2 Split-site scholarships

Split-site scholarships support those undertaking doctoral study at a developing country university, to spend one year at a United Kingdom university as part of their work. The awards were first introduced on a pilot basis in 1998. Each year they are able to make 30–35 awards.

Applicants should be registered for a doctoral degree at their home university. The final qualification obtained will be from the developing country, rather than the UK, institution. The twelve months in the United Kingdom can be taken at any stage in the doctoral study (providing this is justified in the study plan), and can be divided into two or more periods. The scholarship covers full tuition fees for one year at the UK host university, stipend for up to one year in the UK, return air fare and other allowances. The award does not support the period of study at the home country university. Nominations must be received in London by 31 December of the year preceding tenure.

International Awards	Marshall Scholarships

Web site: http://www.marshallscholarship.org/

Marshall Scholarships finance young Americans of high ability to study for a degree in the United Kingdom. At least forty scholars are selected each year to study either at graduate or occasionally undergraduate level at an UK institution in any field of study. Each scholarship is held for two years, but may be renewed at the end of that period.

Marshall Scholarships finance young Americans of high ability to study for a degree in the United Kingdom in a system of higher education recognized for its excellence. Founded by a 1953 Act of Parliament, Marshall Scholarships are mainly funded by the Foreign and Commonwealth Office and commemorate the humane ideals of the Marshall Plan conceived by General George C. Marshall. They express the continuing gratitude of the British people to their American counterparts.

Around forty Marshall Scholarships will be awarded each year. They are tenable at any British university and cover two years of study in any discipline, mostly at graduate level, leading to the award of a British university degree.

Candidates are invited to indicate two preferred universities, although the Marshall Commission reserves the right to decide on final placement. Expressions of interest in studying at universities other than Oxford and Cambridge are particularly welcomed. NB: The selection of scholars is based on a range of factors, including a candidate's choice of course, choice of university, and academic and personal aptitude.

The total value of a Marshall Scholarship varies a little according to the circumstances (place of residence, selected university, etc.) of each scholar but the figure tends on average to be about £20,000 a year. This comprises a personal allowance to cover residence and cost of living expenses at the rate of £654 per month (£815 for scholars at central London institutions), an arrival allowance in the first year of £384, payment of tuition fees, a grant for books of £273, and an annual grant for approved travel in connection with studies, payment of necessary daily expenses in excess of £7.70 a month for travel between place of residence and place of study, provided the distance between the two is reasonable, £260 towards the cost of preparation of any thesis submitted for examination, if required, fares to and from the USA. An amount not exceeding £2220 a year may be added in certain circumstances as a contribution to the support of a dependent spouse. (These figures were for 2005 check for current amounts.)

To qualify for 2006 awards, candidates should be citizens of the United States of America, by the time they take up their scholarship, hold their first undergraduate degree from an accredited four-year college or university in the USA, have obtained a grade point average of not less than 3.7 (or A-) on their undergraduate degree, and not have studied for, or hold a degree or degree-equivalent qualification from a British university.

Resource 5   International Awards

International Awards	Entente Cordiale Scholarships

Web page: http://www.francealacarte.org.uk/entente/

Entente Cordiale scholarships are awarded to outstanding British and French postgraduates, doctoral or post-doctoral students in all subjects to study or undertake research for one academic year on the other side of the Channel. The website includes FAQ, application form and discussion forum.

The Entente Cordiale Scholarships scheme was set up at the time of the 1995 Franco-British summit by Prime Minister John Major and President Jacques Chirac. Now in its eighth year, 23 British and French students are, at the time of writing, studying or undertaking research on the other side of the Channel, making a total of 248 scholars to date.

It is financed entirely by the private sector and by charities.

International Awards	School of Oriental and African Studies Scholarships

Web page: http://www.soas.ac.uk/

SOAS offers two types of named scholarships for its students, available annually:

1 SOAS Felix Scholarship – an award for Indian students applying for a Masters or research (MPhil/PhD) degree. Indian citizens must be under the age of 30, with at least a first-class honours degree. Those who already hold degrees from universities outside India are not eligible to apply. It covers tuition fees at the overseas rate and maintenance of £9936 per annum. Felix scholarships are intended for students who would be unable, without financial assistance, to take up their place. There are six new Felix scholarships available per annum.

2 SOAS Ouseley Memorial Scholarship – an award for a University of London graduate student at SOAS taking a full-time research degree, whose research requires the use of any Middle Eastern or Asian language. Applicants must have applied for a place to study at the School by 31 March in order to be considered for the Ouseley Memorial Scholarship. Its value is a bursary of £6000 for one year only. No remission of tuition fees.

International Awards	EMBL International PHD Programme

Web site: http://www.ebi.ac.uk/training/Studentships/

The EMBL International PhD Programme, originally established in 1983, represents the flagship of (European Molecular Biology Laboratory) EMBL's commitment to first-class training and education. Internationality, dedicated mentoring and early independence in research characterize the programme. Considered to be one of the most competitive PhD training schemes to enter, they are committed to providing EMBL PhD students with the best starting platform for a successful career in science.

The European Bioinformatics Institute (EBI) is a major institute for bioinformatics. It is an outstation of EMBL in Heidelberg, and is responsible, with its international collaborators, for the major databases of nucleic acid and protein sequences and protein structures and is a significant player in research within the field of bioinformatics. It has particularly close contacts with European industry. The EBI is located on the Wellcome Trust Genome Campus, Hinxton, which it shares with the Wellcome Trust's Sanger Institute.

The main annual PhD selection round takes place in spring. Applications open for these selections in July of the previous year and the deadline for applications is November.

International Awards	Leibniz Scholarship

Web page: http://london.daad.de/

Deutscher Akademischer Austausch Dienst (German Academic Exchange Service)

London Funding Programmes for Germany Leibniz Scholarship

The programme is open to graduates, PhD students and post-docs from around the world. Scholarships can be awarded for a period from 6 to 36 months. It is also possible to gain a doctorate in Germany. The research topics are specified by the institutes themselves. Go to the web page to see the subject areas currently available. Leibniz Institutes are non-university research and service facilities which are organized in the Leibniz Association (WGL). Detailed information about the Leibniz Association and its institutes is available at the following web site: www.leibniz-gemeinschaft.de. Applications for a 'DAAD-Leibniz Scholarship' should be submitted to the DAAD London office. Funding ranges from €795 to €1840.

Resource 5 International Awards

RESOURCE 6

STUDENT VISA GUIDE	

International students must also obtain student visas to allow them to enter the UK as PhD students. There are many complex rules, and these sometimes change, so you must visit the web site for the most current information. However, this section reproduces some of the information from the UK government about student visa regulations, which were valid in 2005. It also provides details of web sites that provide further information and help.

Resource 6   Student Visa Guide

STUDENT VISA GUIDE	UK Student Visas

For the most recent regulations it is important that you visit the web page: http://www.ukvisas.gov.uk/students

(and look for 'student visas', document INF 5).

The UK immigration rules have a habit of changing quite frequently and the details are not always clear until very close to the actual date of their introduction. Also note that conditions for applying for a visa vary considerably around the world and any potential applicant should visit the web site of, or contact, their UK mission for up-to-date information well in advance of applying for a visa (www.fco.gov.uk/embassies). Students particularly can find themselves in trouble when they apply for a visa a short time before their studies are due to begin and then find that the waiting time is much longer than they expected.

How do I qualify to travel to the UK as a student?

You must be able to show that you have been accepted on a course of study at an educational establishment that is on the UK's Department for Education and Skills (DfES) Register of Education and Training Providers. Contact details for the DfES are near the end of this guidance or you can search the register on the DfES web site at www.dfes.gov.uk/providersregister

You must be able to show that you are going to follow:

- a recognized full-time degree course; or

- a course run during the week involving at least 15 hours of organized daytime study each week; or

- a full-time course at an independent fee-paying school.

You must also:

- be able to pay for your course and support yourself and any dependants, and live in the UK without working or any help from public funds; and

- intend to leave the UK when you complete your studies.

If you are a degree student and you successfully complete your studies, you may be able to take work permit employment if you meet the requirements. You can get more information about work permits in the work permit holders (INF 13) guidance note.

If you graduate in an approved science or engineering subject you can apply to stay in the UK, to look for or to take work, for an additional year after your degree course finishes without getting a work permit. For more information, please see the permit-free employment (INF 14) guidance note. Under the 'Fresh Talent: Working in Scotland' scheme, if you successfully complete a degree-level course or above, and it was awarded by a Scottish institution, you may be able to live and work in Scotland for up to two years after achieving your qualification.

What is a visa?

A visa is a certificate that is put into your passport or travel document by an Entry Clearance Officer at a British mission overseas. The visa gives you permission to enter the UK.

Resource 6 Student Visa Guide

If you have a valid UK visa, you will not normally be refused entry to the UK unless your circumstances have changed, or you gave false information or did not reveal important facts when you applied for your visa.

When you arrive in the UK, an Immigration Officer may question you, so take all relevant documents in your hand luggage.

Do I need a visa to study in the UK?

You will need a visa if you:

- are a national of one of the countries listed at the end of this guidance;

- are stateless (you do not have a nationality);

- hold a non-national travel document; or

- hold a passport issued by an authority not recognized by the UK.

Nationals from 10 non-visa countries (Australia, Canada, Hong Kong (but not British Nationals (Overseas)), Japan, Malaysia, New Zealand, Singapore, South Africa, South Korea and the USA) now need an entry clearance if they are staying longer than six months. At the moment, other non-visa nationals do not need to have an entry clearance to study in the UK.

In 2005 legislation was introduced to make sure that all non-European Union and non-European Economic Area (EEA) nationals wanting to stay for longer than six months will need an entry clearance.

If you do not need an entry clearance when you arrive in the UK, you will have to satisfy the Immigration Officer that you qualify for entry. They will then give you permission to stay in the UK for six months. You will not be allowed to extend your stay in the UK as a student unless you arrived with a student or prospective student visa, or are studying on a course at degree level or higher.

To extend your stay you will need to apply for a residence permit at the Immigration and Nationality Directorate (contact details are at the end of this guidance). They will charge you a fee for this.

You should apply for a visa before you travel to the UK.

How do I apply for a visa?

You will need to fill in a visa application form (VAF 1 – non-settlement). You can download the form from the web site, or get one free of charge from your nearest British mission overseas where there is a visa section.

You can apply for a visit visa at any full service visa-issuing office. For all other types of visa, you should apply in the country of which you are a national, or where you legally live.

You can apply in a number of ways, for example by post, by courier, in person and online. The visa section will tell you about the ways in which you can apply. In some countries, if you are applying for a visa to stay in the UK for more than six months, you may need to be tested for active tuberculosis before your application is accepted, You can find out if you need to be tested by using the 'do I need a UK visa?' link on the web site given at the beginning, or by contacting your nearest British mission overseas where there is a visa section.

Resource 6   Student Visa Guide

What will I need to make my application?

To apply for a visa you will need the following.

- Application form VAF1 – non-settlement available online here: http://www.fco.gov.uk/Files/kfile/VAF1,1.pdf which you have filled in correctly;

- Your passport or travel document;

- A recent passport-sized (45mm x 35mm), colour photograph of yourself. This should be:

  - taken against a light-coloured background,

  - clear and of good quality, and not framed or backed,

  - printed on normal photographic paper; and,

  - full face and without sunglasses, hat or other head covering unless you wear this for cultural or religious reasons;

- The visa fee. This cannot be refunded and you must normally pay it in the local currency of the country where you are applying.

- Supporting documents relevant to your application.

What supporting documents should I include with my application?

You should include all the documents you can to show that you qualify for entry to the UK as a student. If you do not, your application may be refused.

As a guide, you should include:

- any relevant diplomas or educational certificates;

- a letter from the university, college or school confirming that you have been accepted on a course of study in the UK, and statement of charges for the course;

- evidence of government sponsorship (if appropriate).

You may also need to show:

- bank statements, payslips or other evidence to show that you can pay for your stay and your course of studies in the UK, and

- a letter from your host or sponsor in the UK to say that they will support you and provide accommodation for you during your studies, with evidence that they can do so.

Your application will be refused if any documents are forged.

What will happen when I make my application?

The Entry Clearance Officer will try to make a decision using your application form and the supporting documents you have provided. If this is not possible, they will need to interview you.

Check your visa when you get it. You should make sure that:

- your personal details are correct;

- it correctly states the purpose for which you want to come to the UK, and

Resource 6 Student Visa Guide

- it is valid for the date on which you want to travel. (You can ask for it to be post-dated for up to three months if you do not plan to travel immediately.)

If you think there is anything wrong with your visa, contact the visa section immediately.

What are public funds?

Under the immigration rules if you want to travel to the UK you must be able to support yourself and live without claiming certain state benefits (see the web page for more details).

Can I extend my stay as a student?

If you enter the UK with a student or prospective student visa, or you want to study on a course at degree level or higher, you can apply for an extension of stay to the Immigration and Nationality Directorate, which is a part of the Home Office. (Contact details are at end of this guidance.) The Immigration and Nationality Directorate will charge you a fee for any extension to your stay.

The maximum period of time that a student can stay in the UK on short courses one after the other, below degree level, is two years.

If you did not enter the UK with a student or prospective student visa or are not studying on a degree level course or higher, you will not be allowed to extend your stay.

Can I work?

You can take part-time or holiday work, but you must not:

- work for more than 20 hours per week during term time unless your placement is part of your studies, has been agreed with your education institution and leads to a degree or qualification awarded by a nationally recognized examining body;

- do business, be self-employed or provide services as a professional sports person or entertainer; or

- work full-time in a permanent job.

If you are coming to the UK as a student for six months or less, you must ask the Entry Clearance Officer for permission to work.

Can I switch to work permit employment when I am in the UK?

You may be able to switch if:

- you have completed a recognized degree course at either a UK publicly-funded institution of further or higher education, or an approved private education institution that has satisfactory records of enrolment and attendance;

- you hold a valid work permit for employment;

- you have the written consent of any government or agency that is sponsoring you; and

- you have not broken immigration law.

Can I bring my husband, or wife and children with me?

Your husband or wife and any of your children under 18 can come to the UK with you during your studies, as long as you can support them and live without needing help from public funds.

Will my husband or wife be allowed to work?

Your husband or wife will be allowed to work in the UK if we give you permission to stay in the country for 12 months or more.

Can I go to the UK to arrange my studies?

You can travel to the UK as a prospective student for up to six months to arrange your studies. You will need to show that:

- you intend to enrol on a course of study within six months of arriving in the UK;

- you can pay for your course, support yourself and your dependants, and live without working or needing any help from public funds; and

- you intend to leave the UK when you finish your studies or when your permission to stay ends if you do not qualify to stay in the UK as a student.

Note: You should not buy a ticket, or pay all or part of the cost of a study course if your visa application being delayed or refused would mean that you lose your money.

When should I apply?

You should apply in good time for your entry clearance so that you are not delayed in getting into the UK. It can get very busy in visa sections, especially over the summer when lots of students are applying.

More advice and information

You can get more advice about studying in the UK from:

UKCOSA

The Council for International Education (UKCOSA) provides advice and information to international students studying or planning to study in the UK, their family, teachers and other advisers:

The Council for International Education

9–17 St Albans Place

London N1 0NX

Web site: http://www.ukcosa.org.uk

Resource 6 Student Visa Guide

British Council

The British Council provides information to help international students prepare for study in the UK. This link will take you to the British Council's 'First Steps' guidance on preparing for entry clearance:

http://britishcouncil.org/Feducation/Fqdu/
FPreparing_for_entry_clearance_202003–2004_English.pdf

First Steps Guidance – Preparing for entry clearance

More information about studying in the UK is available from:

The British Council

Bridgewater House

58 Whitworth Street

Manchester M1 6BB

Web site: www.britcoun.org/education/qdu/index.htm

UK visas

You can get more advice and information about visas from:

UKvisas

London SW1A 2AH

General enquiries: (+44) (0)20 7008 8438

Application forms: (+44) (0)20 7008 8308

Web site: www.ukvisas.gov.uk/enquiries

Immigration and Nationality Directorate (IND)

You can get more advice and information about extending your stay once you are in the UK from:

Immigration and Nationality Directorate

Croydon Public Caller Unit

Lunar House

40 Wellesley Road

Croydon CR9 2BY

General enquiries: (+44) (0)870 606 7766

Application forms: (+44) (0)870 241 0645

E-mail: indpublicenquiries@ind.homeoffice.gsi.gov.uk

Web site: http://www.ind.homeoffice.gov.uk

Resource 6 Student Visa Guide

Immigration Advisory Service

The IAS is an independent charity that gives confidential advice and help, and can represent people who are applying for a visa for the UK.

Immigration Advisory Service

3rd Floor, County House

190 Great Dover Street

London SE1 4YB

Phone: (+44) (0)20 7967 1200

Duty Office (24 hrs): (+44) (0)20 8814 1559

Fax: (+44) (0)20 7403 5875

E-mail: advice@iasuk.org

Web site: http://www.iasuk.org

HM Revenue and Customs

Advice on bringing personal belongings and goods into the United Kingdom can be obtained from:

HM Revenue & Customs

Dorset House

Stamford Street

London SE1 9PY

Phone: (+44) (0)845 010 9000

Web site: http://www.hmrc.gov.uk

Health insurance

If you come from a country with a health-care agreement with the UK, or you are enrolled on a course for more than six months, you may be able to get medical treatment on the National Health Service (NHS). Short-term students who are in the UK for six months or less are not entitled to free medical treatment, and you will have to pay for any treatment you get. Please make sure you have enough health insurance for the whole of your stay.

Drugs warning

Anyone found smuggling drugs into the UK will face serious penalties. Drug traffickers may try to bribe travellers. If you are travelling to the United Kingdom avoid any involvement with drugs.

Resource 6 Student Visa Guide

Forged or destroyed documents

Travellers to the UK may commit an offence if they do not produce valid travel documents or passports for themselves and their children. People found guilty of

this offence face up to two years in prison or a fine (or both).

List of visa nationals

If you are a national of one of the countries listed in the link below, or if you are stateless, hold a non-national travel document or passport issued by an authority not recognized by the UK, you must hold a valid UK visa on each* occasion that you travel to the UK. Use this link to see a list of visa nationals:

http://www.ukvisas.gov.uk (search for 'Visa Nationals').

*Visas are not required if you are settled in the UK or if you already have permission to stay in the UK and are returning to the UK before your permission to stay expires.

If you are not a visa national you do not need a visa to enter the UK as a visitor. You may need to apply for prior entry clearance if you wish to come to the UK for another reason.

Resource 6 Student Visa Guide

RESOURCE 7

Directory	

The final resource provides a list of UK university web sites, charity web sites, UK and EU Research Council and research agency web sites, and some helpful web sites to provide extra information and advice on anything else you still want to know.

Directory	UK University web pages
University of Oxford	http://www.ox.ac.uk/
University of Cambridge	http://www.cam.ac.uk/
University of St. Andrews	http://www.st-andrews.ac.uk/
University of Glasgow	http://www.gla.ac.uk/
University of Aberdeen	http://www.abdn.ac.uk/
University of London	http://www.lon.ac.uk
University of Durham	http://www.dur.ac.uk/
University of Birmingham	http://www.bham.ac.uk/
University of Bristol	http://www.bristol.ac.uk/
University of Leeds	http://www.leeds.ac.uk/
University of Liverpool	http://www.liv.ac.uk/
University of Manchester	http://www.manchester.ac.uk/
University of Sheffield	http://www.sheffield.ac.uk/
University of Wales, Aberystwyth	http://www.aber.ac.uk/
University of Reading	http://www.reading.ac.uk/
Queen's University, Belfast	http://www.qub.ac.uk/
University of Exeter	http://www.ex.ac.uk/
University of Newcastle upon Tyne	http://www.ncl.ac.uk/
University of Nottingham	http://www.nottingham.ac.uk/
University of Southhampton	http://www.soton.ac.uk/
Brunel University	http://www.brunel.ac.uk/
Heriot-Watt University	http://www.hw.ac.uk/
University of Bath	http://www.bath.ac.uk/
University of Bradford	http://www.bradford.ac.uk/
University of East Anglia	http://www.uea.ac.uk/
University of Essex	http://www.essex.ac.uk/
University of Kent	http://www.kent.ac.uk/
Keele University	http://www.keele.ac.uk/
University of Lancaster	http://www.lancs.ac.uk/
Loughborough University	http://www.lboro.ac.uk/
University of Stirling	http://www.stirling.ac.uk/
University of Sussex	http://www.sussex.ac.uk/

Resource 7 Directory

University of Warwick	http://www.warwick.ac.uk/
University of Ulster	http://www.ulst.ac.uk/
University of York	http://www.york.ac.uk/
Open University	http://www.open.ac.uk/
Abertay University	http://www.abertay.ac.uk/
Anglia Polytechnic University	http://www.apu.ac.uk/
University of Brighton	http://www.brighton.ac.uk/
Bournemouth University	http://www.bournemouth.ac.uk/
University of Central England	http://www.uce.ac.uk/
University of Central Lancashire	http://www.uclan.ac.uk/
Coventry University	http://www.coventry.ac.uk/
University of Derby	http://www.derby.ac.uk/
De Montfort University	http://www.dmu.ac.uk/
University of East London	http://www.uel.ac.uk/
University of Glamorgan	http://www.glam.ac.uk/
Glasgow Caledonian University	http://www.gcal.ac.uk/
University of Greenwich	http://www.gre.ac.uk/
University of Hertfordshire	http://www.herts.ac.uk/
University of Huddersfield	http://www.hud.ac.uk/
Kingston University	http://www.kingston.ac.uk/
Leeds Metropolitan University	http://www.lmu.ac.uk/
University of Lincoln	http://www.lincoln.ac.uk/
Liverpool John Moores University	http://www.livjm.ac.uk/
London Metropolitan University	http://www.londonmet.ac.uk/
University of Luton	http://www.luton.ac.uk/
Manchester Metropolitan University	http://www.mmu.ac.uk/
Middlesex University	http://www.mdx.ac.uk/
Napier University	http://www.napier.ac.uk/
University of Northumbria	http://www.unn.ac.uk/
Nottingham Trent University	http://www.ntu.ac.uk/
Oxford Brookes University	http://www.brookes.ac.uk/
University of Paisley	http://www.paisley.ac.uk/
University of Plymouth	http://www.plymouth.ac.uk/

Resource 7 Directory
UK universities

University of Portsmouth	http://www.port.ac.uk/
Sheffield Hallam University	http://www.shu.ac.uk/
South Bank University	http://www.lsbu.ac.uk/
Staffordshire University	http://www.staffs.ac.uk/
University of Sunderland	http://www.sunderland.ac.uk/
University of Teesside	http://www.tees.ac.uk/
Thames Valley University	http://www.tvu.ac.uk/
Robert Gordon University	http://www.rgu.ac.uk/
University of the West of England	http://www.uwe.ac.uk
University of Westminster	http://www.wmin.ac.uk/
University of Wolverhampton	http://ww.wlv.ac.uk/

Resource 7 Directory
UK charities

Directory	Charity web pages
Association of Medical Research Charities	http://www.amrc.org.uk/
Charity Choice	http://www.charitychoice.co.uk/
Charities Direct	http://www.charitiesdirect.com/
CharityNet	http://www.charitynet.org/
The Charity Commission	http://www.charity-commission.gov.uk/
The Carnegie Trust	http://www.carnegie-trust.org/
Jerwood Foundation	http://www.jerwood.org/
Joseph Rowntree Foundation	http://www.jrf.org.uk/
The Leverhulme Trust	http:// www.leverhulme.org.uk/
Action Cancer	http://www.actioncancer.org/
Action Medical Research	http://www.action.org.uk/
Action on Addiction	http://www.aona.co.uk/
Alzheimer's Research Trust	http://www.alzheimers-research.org.uk/
Alzheimer's Society	http://www.alzheimers.org.uk/
Arthritis Research Campaign	http://www.arc.org.uk/
Association for International Cancer Research	http://www.aicr.org.uk/
Association for Spina Bifida and Hydrocephalus	http://www.asbah.org/
Asthma UK	http://www.asthma.org.uk/
Ataxia – Telangiectasia Society	http://www.ataxia.org.uk/
Ataxia UK	http://www.atsociety.org.uk/
BackCare	http://www.backpain.org/
Bardhan Research and Education Trust of Rotherham	http://beehive.thisisgloucestershire.co.uk/
Barnwood House Trust	http://www.barnwoodhousetrust.org/
Blackie Foundation Trust	http://www.blackieft.org/
Brain Research Trust	http://www.brt.org.uk/
Breakthrough Breast Cancer	http://www.breakthrough.org.uk/
Breast Cancer Campaign	http://www.bcc-uk.org/

British Council for Prevention of Blindness	http://www.bcpb.org/
British Eye Research Foundation (now merged with Fight for Sight)	http://www.berf.org.uk/
British Heart Foundation	http://www.bhf.org.uk/
British Liver Trust	http://www.britishlivertrust.org.uk/
British Lung Foundation	http://www.lunguk.org/
British Occupational Health Research Foundation	http://www.bohrf.org.uk/
British Retinitis Pigmentosa Society	http://www.brps.org.uk/
British Sjögren's Syndrome Association	http://www.bssa.uk.net/
British Skin Foundation	http://www.britishskinfoundation.org.uk/
British Vascular Foundation (now merged with the Vascular Society)	http://www.bvf.org.uk/
BUPA Foundation	http://www.bupafoundation.org/
Cancer Research UK	http://www.cancerresearchuk.org/
CFS Research Foundation	http://www.cfsresearchfoundation.org.uk/
Chest, Heart and Stroke Scotland	http://www.chss.org.uk/
Children with Leukaemia	http://www.leukaemia.org/
Children's Liver Disease Foundation	http://www.childliverdisease.org/
Chronic Disease Research Foundation	http://www.cdrf.org.uk/
Chronic Granulomatous Disorder Research Trust	http://www.cgd.org.uk/
Core (The Digestive Disorders Foundation)	http://www.digestivedisorders.org.uk/
Cystic Fibrosis Trust	http://www.cftrust.org.uk/
Deafness Research UK	http://www.deafnessresearch.org.uk/
Diabetes Research & Wellness Foundation	http://www.diabeteswellnessnet.org.uk/

Resource 7 Directory
UK charities

Diabetes UK	http://www.diabetes.org.uk/
Dystrophic Epidermolysis Bullosa Research Association	http://www.debra.org.uk/
EMF Biological Research Trust	http://www.emfbrt.org/
Epilepsy Research Foundation	http://www.erf.org.uk/
Foundation for Liver Research	http://www.ucl.ac.uk/liver-research/
Foundation for the Study of Infant Deaths	http://sids.org.uk/fsid/
Fund for Epilepsy	http://www.epilepsyfund.org.uk/
Guy's and St Thomas' Charity	http://www.gsttcharity.org.uk/
Healing Foundation	http://www.thehealingfoundation.org
Health Foundation	http://www.health.org.uk/
Heart Research UK	http://www.heartresearch.org.uk/
Huntington's Disease Association	http://www.hda.org.uk/
Hypertension Trust	http://www.hypertensiontrust.org/
Inspire Foundation	http://www.inspire-foundation.org.uk/
International Spinal Research Trust	http://www.spinal-research.org/
Juvenile Diabetes Research Foundation	http://www.jdrf.org.uk/
Lister Institute of Preventive Medicine	http://www.lister-institute.org.uk/
Little Foundation	http://www.thelittlefoundation.org.uk/
Ludwig Institute for Cancer Research	http://www.licr.org/
Marie Curie Research Institute	http://www.mcri.ac.uk/default.html
Mason Medical Research Foundation	http://www.cmmrf.org/
Meningitis Research Foundation	http://www.meningitis.org.uk/
Meningitis Trust	http://www.meningitis-trust.org.uk/
Migraine Trust	http://www.migrainetrust.org/
Motor Neurone Disease Association	http://www.mndassociation.org/

Multiple Sclerosis Society of Great Britain and Northern Ireland	http://www.mssociety.org.uk/
Muscular Dystrophy Campaign	http://www.muscular-dystrophy.org/
Myasthenia Gravis Association	http://www.mgauk.org/
National Association for Colitis & Crohn's Disease	http://www.nacc.org.uk/
National Eczema Society	http://www.eczema.org/
National Endometriosis Society	http://www.endo.org.uk/
National Eye Research Centre	http://www.nerc.co.uk/
National Kidney Research Fund	http://www.nkrf.org.uk/
National Osteoporosis Society	http://www.nos.org.uk/
Neuro-Disability Research Trust	http://www.neuro-disability.org.uk/
North West Cancer Research Fund	http://www.cancerresearchnorthwest.co.uk/
Northern Ireland Chest, Heart and Stroke Association	http://www.nichsa.com/
Northern Ireland Leukaemia Research Fund	http://www.leukaemia-ni.org/
Novartis Foundation	http://www.novartisfound.org.uk/
Novo Nordisk UK Research Foundation	http://www.novonordiskfoundation.co.uk/
Nuffield Foundation	http://www.nuffieldfoundation.org/
Parkinson's Disease Society of the UK	http://www.parkinsons.org.uk/
PBC Foundation (UK) Ltd, The	http://www.pbcfoundation.org.uk/
Primary Immunodeficiency Association	http://www.pia.org.uk/
Progressive Supranuclear Palsy Association, The	http://www.pspeur.org/
Psoriasis Association	http://www.psoriasis-association.org.uk/
Queen Victoria Hospital Blond McIndoe Research Foundation	http://www.blondmcindoe.com/
RAFT – The Restoration of Appearance and Function Trust	http://www.raft.ac.uk/

Remedi	http://www.remedi.org.uk/
Research Into Ageing	http://www.ageing.org/
Royal College of Surgeons of England	http://www.rcseng.ac.uk/
Scottish Hospital Endowments Research Trust	http://www.shert.co.uk/
Sir Jules Thorn Charitable Trust	http://www.julesthorntrust.org.uk/
Society for Endocrinology	http://www.endocrinology.org/
SPARKS (Sport Aiding Medical Research for Kids)	http://www.sparks.org.uk/
Spencer Dayman Meningitis UK	http://www.spencerdayman.org.uk/
St Peter's Trust for Kidney, Bladder & Prostate Research	http://www.ucl.ac.uk/uro-neph/spt
Stroke Association, The	http://www.stroke.org.uk/
Tenovus	http://www.tenovus.org.uk/
Tommy's The Baby Charity	http://www.tommys.org/
Tuberous Sclerosis Association	http://www.tuberous-sclerosis.org/
Tyneside Leukaemia Research Association	http://www.tlra.co.uk/
Ulster Cancer Foundation	http://www.ulstercancer.org/
Wellbeing of Women	http://www.wellbeingofwomen.org.uk/
WellChild (registered as The WellChild Trust)	http://www.wellchild.org.uk/
Wellcome Trust, The	http://www.wellcome.ac.uk/
Wessex Medical Trust	http://www.hope.org.uk/
William Harvey Research Foundation	http://www.whrf.org.uk/
World Cancer Research Fund	http://www.wcrf-uk.org/
Yorkshire Cancer Research	http://www.ycr.org.uk/

Resource 7 Directory
research agencies

Directory	Research Agency web pages
http://www.research-councils.ac.uk/	
The Research Council (RCUK) web site provides a gateway into the seven councils' web sites plus information about cross-council activities.	
http://www.ahrc.ac.uk/	
Arts and Humanities Research Council (AHRC)	
http://www.bbsrc.ac.uk/	
Biotechnology and Biological Sciences Research Council (BBSRC)	
http://www.epsrc.ac.uk/	
Engineering and Physical Science Research Council (EPSRC)	
http://www.esrc.ac.uk/	
Economic and Social Research Council (ESRC)	
http://www.mrc.ac.uk/	
Medical Research Council (MRC)	
http://www.nerc.ac.uk/	
Natural Environment Research Council (NERC)	
http://www.pparc.ac.uk/	
Particle Physics and Astronomy Research Council (PPARC)	
http://www.cclrc.ac.uk/	
Council for the Central Laboratory of the Research Councils (CCLRC)	
http://www.britishcouncil.org/	
The British Council	
http://www.britac.ac.uk/	
The British Academy (The National Academy for Humanities and Social Sciences)	
http://www.nesta.org/	
National Endowment for Science, Technology and the Arts (NESTA)	
http:// www.nlcb.org.uk/	
UK National Lottery Charities Council. (Community Fund which gives Lottery money to charities and voluntary and community groups)	
http:// www.sciart.org/	
SCIART (Encourages creative and experimental collaborations between scientists and artists, which further enhance the public engagement with both science and art)	

Resource 7 Directory information & advice

http://europa.eu.int/

EUROPA (The European Union online)

http://www.esf.org/

European Science Foundation (ESF)

http://cordis.europa.eu.int/

CORDIS (European Community Research & Development Information Service)

Directory	Information and advice
http://www.ukro.ac.uk/	
	Information and advice service for EU research and higher education.
http://www.scholarship-search.org.uk/	
	Advice and assistance on scholarships with online eligibility testers.
http://www.support4learning.org.uk/money/postgraduate_and_mba_study.cfm	
	Support for Learning. A list of useful links to funding opportunities. This site is produced and maintained by HERO, who also produce the Higher Education and Research Opportunities in the UK (HERO) web site and the Aimhigher student portal.
http://www.hero.ac.uk/	
	Higher Education and Research Opportunities in the UK – university guide with performance tables.
http://www.aimhigher.ac.uk/	
	The Aimhigher portal. General advice about higher education in the UK.
http://www.egas-online.org/fwa/	
	Educational Grants Advisory Service with downloadable guide to student funding.
http://www.grad.ac.uk/	
	The UK GRAD programme.
http://www.newroutephd.ac.uk/	
	Full information on New Route PhDs™.
http://www.npc.org.uk/essentials/publications	
	National Graduate Committee information for postgraduate students.
http://www.direct.gov.uk/EducationAndLearning/UniversityAndHigherEducation/fs/en	
	UK government assistance about higher education in the UK.
http://www.educationuk.org/	
	British Council information and advice for foreign students wishing to study in the UK.
http://www.ukcosa.org.uk/pages/advice.htm	
	The Council for International Education frequently asked questions for international students wishing to study in the UK.
http://www.skill.org.uk/info/infosheets/pg_ed.doc	
	Factsheet for students with disabilities wishing to obtain funding and study in the UK, produced by the National Bureau for Students with Disabilities.

Resource 7 Directory information & advice

Index

accommodation
  university, 52, 56, 70, 102,
    110–111
  private, 111–115
  shared, 111
  also see tenancy agreement
administration, 53, 55, 104,
  118–119
aerospace, 147
agriculture, 150, 151
agri-food, 31
Alex Dent, 79
alternative energy production,
  32
ancient universities, 51
animal sciences, 31
application form
  for ORSAS, 38, 153–159
  for PhD, 70, 84, 90–95
applying for PhD, 49–55
applying for funding, see
  funding
architecture, 14, 19, 149, 151,
  152
arts, *see* creative arts & design
arts and humanities, 16, 17, 19,
  21–23
  see also creative arts and
    design
Arts and Humanities Research
  Council (AHRC), 31,184
arthritis and rheumatism, 34,
  40, 141
Arthritis Research Campaign, 40,
  141, 178
asthma and other respiratory
  disorders, 34, 40, 178
Ataxia Fund, 141

authorship, 120–121
biochemistry and cell biology,
  31
bioinformatics, 32, 164
biological sciences, 19, 31, 58,
  63, 149, 150, 151, 184
biomolecular sciences, 31
biophysics, 32
bioscience engineering, 32
Biotechnology and Biological
  Sciences Research Council
  (BBSRC), 31–32, 134, 184
British Academy, 183
British Antarctic Survey, 34, 134
British Chevening Scholarships,
  161
British Consulate, 105
British Council, 48–49, 133, 161,
  162, 171, 184
British Embassy, 105, 161
British Geological Survey, 34
British Heart Foundation, 40,
  141, 178
British High Commission, 105
British Marshall Scholarships,
  39, 154, 163
budget
  for research, 30, 38, 39
  your own, 108–109, 118
building & planning, 149, 151,
  152
business & administrative
  studies, 149, 150, 151, 152
campus-based universities, 52,
  53, 55, 110–111
Caledonian Research Foundation and Carnegie Trust,
  140, 178

cancer and cell proliferation, 25,
28, 34, 40, 41, 42, 61, 63,
64, 82, 134, 142, 178, 179,
180, 181, 182, 183
Cancer Research UK, 41, 134,
142, 179
cell biology, development and
growth, 31, 34
Centre
Climate & Land Surface
Systems Interaction, 35
Data Assimilation Research,
35
for Ecology & Hydrology, 34
Environmental Systems
Science, 35
for Innovative and Collaborative
Engineering, 147
Joint Astronomy, 35
National Oceanography, 34
NERC for Atmospheric Science,
35
for Observation and Modelling
of Earthquakes & Tectonics,
35
of Observation of Air-Sea
Interactions & Fluxes, 35
for Polar Observation &
Modelling, 35
for Population Biology, 35
for Terrestrial Carbon Dynamics,
35
Tyndall, 35
UK Astronomy Technology, 35
CERN, 32
changing your supervisor, 8, 75,
80
charities, 30, 40–42, 47, 129,
130, 133, 139–144, 164, 178
charity webpages, 178–183
chemistry, 6, 8, 33, 63, 73, 134
children and adolescents, 25,
34, 41, 106, 110, 162, 171,
173, 179
circulatory diseases, 34
city-based universities, 50, 55,
59, 110
cognitive systems, 32
Commonwealth Scholarships
and Fellowships Plan, 162

Commonwealth Scholarship
Commission (CSC), 37, 162
communication, 18, 26, 33, 67,
81, 108, 126–128
communication technologies,
see information and
communication technolo-
gies
computer science, 1, 6, 8, 19,
67, 130, 149, 150, 151, 152
conference paper, 57, 59, 62,
100, 116
conference trips, 101, 137
contacting a supervisor, 67–71
context, 17, 19, 22
CORDIS, 185
cosmic rays, 35
Council for the Central
Laboratory of the Research
Councils (CCLRC), 32, 62,
183
Council for International
Education (UKCOSA), 171,
185
courses, 1, 8, 11, 13, 31, 43, 46,
53, 60, 67, 73, 76, 84, 101,
118, 128, 145–146
creative arts & design, 14, 16,
17, 19, 21–23, 25, 31, 149,
152, 154, 183, 184
credit, 121
critical review, 15, 19, 25, 57,
59, 73, 121
CV (Curriculum Vitae), 67, 69,
70, 97, 98
cynicism, 6, 10, 17, 23, 82,
116–117
debt, 4, 27, 44, 55, 58, 109
dentistry, see oral health
Department for Education and
Skills (DfES), 37, 154, 167
Department for Trade and
Industry (DTI), 30
design, see creative arts and
design
diabetes, 34, 41, 137, 179, 180
directory, 175–186
doctorate
first-degree, first professional,
12
higher, 12–13

doctorate – *contd*
  junior, ordinary, 12
  practical, 13, 15, 24
  professional, taught, 13, 15
  types of, 11–15
doctor
  medical, 1, 14
  of philosophy, *see* doctor-
    ate, PhD
documentation
  of research, 18, 117
  for visa application, 104–106,
    169
Dorothy Hodgkin Postgraduate
  Award, 154, 160
DPhil, *see* doctorate, PhD
Economic and Social Research
  Council (ESRC), 32–33, 184
economic performance and
  development, 33
education, 14, 28, 29, 64, 133,
  149, 150, 151, 152, 178
Educational Grants Advisory
  Service, 184
electronics, 32, 148
eligibility
  English language, 7, 90
  for funding, 36, 37, 38, 45–49,
    90
  for PhD, 6
  for studentships, 45–49,
    145–146
email, 67–70, 91
EMBL International PhD
  Programme, 164–165
EngD, *see* Engineering Doctorate
EngD centres, 146–149
engineering, 11, 13, 19, 31, 32,
  33, 40, 137, 145–146
engineering and biological
  systems, 31
Engineering and Physical
  Sciences Research Council
  (EPSRC), 33, 39, 145, 160,
  183
Engineering Doctorate (EngD),
  1, 7, 11, 15, 43, 46,
  145–149
  see also doctorate, PhD
English language and literature,
  31

English language proficiency, *see*
  eligibility
Entente Cordiale Scholarships,
  163–164
environment and human
  behaviour, 33
EU (European Union), *see* fees,
  funding, scholarships,
  studentships
EUROPA (the European Union
  on-line), 184
European Community Research
  and Development Information Service (CORDIS), 185
European Science Foundation
  (ESF), 185
evidence, 17, 19, 22, 23, 25, 82,
  83, 88, 121, 124
  for visa application, 104,
    106, 169
example
  completed ORSAS form, *see*
    Overseas Research
    Students Awards Scheme
  offer letter, *see* offer letter
  log book page, *see* log book
  research proposals, *see*
    research proposal
  tenancy agreement, *see*
    tenancy agreement
experience of a supervisor,
  75–77
exploring our solar system, 35
fees, 2, 23, 24, 27, 90, 96, 98,
  99, 100, 102, 103, 104, 105,
  106, 108, 109, 118, 136,
  140, 141, 142, 143
  for EU citizens, 28, 29, 36, 39,
    45
  home, *see* for UK citizens
  international, 28, 29, 30, 37,
    38, 42, 47, 48, 153, 154
  for part-time students, 24
  for UK citizens, 24, 28, 29, 36,
    39, 45
  university, 27, 28, 29, 56
finding a supervisor, 66–67
first-year viva, 73
foreign, *see* international
formulation engineering, 147
Fulbright Scholarships, 39
full-time, *see* studying

fundamental particles of nature, 35
funding
 applying for, 30, 39, 44, 47, 50, 71, 90, 153, 164
 British Council, 48–49, 133, 161, 162, 171–172, 184, 186
 charities, 30, 40–42, 47, 133–134, 139–144
 CSC, *see* Commonwealth Scholarship Commission
 EU, 37–39, 40–44, 45–48, 132–135, 145–152
 home, *see* UK
 industrial, 43–44, 46–48, 132–135
 international, 37–39, 40–42, 48–49, 132–135, 153–165
 non-UK, *see* EU and international
 ORSAS, *see* Overseas Research Students Awards Scheme
 UK, 30–37, 40–44, 45–48, 132–135, 145–15
general studentship webpages, 133
genes and developmental biology, 31
genetics, molecular structure and dynamics, 33, 63
glass-plate universities, 52–53
governance and citizenship, 33
graduate application form, *see* application form for PhD
gravitational waves, 35
Great Britain Sasakawa Foundation, 137
grid computing, 35
ground and space-based facilities, 35
halls, *see* university accommodation
health of elderly people, 34
HEFCE research performance indicators, 64, 65, 184
help, *see* information and advice webpages
Higher Education and Research Opportunities (HERO), 63, 186
HM Revenue and Customs, 173

home fees, *see* fees
housing, *see* accommodation
humanities, *see* arts and humanities
hypothesis, 19, 21, 25, 88, 124
Immigration Advisory Service (IAS), 172
Immigration and Nationality Directorate (IND), 172
immunology and infection, 33
infections, 34
information and advice webpages, 186
information and communication technologies, *see* communication technologies
infrastructure and environment, 33
innovative manufacturing, 33
insomnia, 124–125
interests, 7–8, 37, 45, 46, 47, 57, 60, 67, 71, 76, 78
international, *see* fees, funding, scholarships, visa
internet, 129–131
 see also webpages
interview, 36, 56, 57, 71, 91, 96–102, 104
interview questions, 98–100
ISIS, 32
justification, 20
knowledge, communication and learning, 33
landlord, 111–113
languages, 14, 17, 31, 111, 150
law, 13, 14, 31, 151, 152
learning, 11, 12, 17, 20, 24, 25, 26, 33, 54, 55, 117, 123, 126
Leibniz Scholarship, 165
Leukaemia Research Fund, 142
loans, 28, 48, 118
log book, 73, 74
logical argument, 19–20
librarianship, information and museum studies, 31, 151
life sciences interface, 33
lifecourse, family and generations, 33

manufacturing systems
engineering, 147, 149
marine technology, 35, 150
Marshall Scholarships, 39, 154,
163
materials, 32, 33, 147, 148
mathematical sciences, 6, 16,
17, 21, 33, 40, 73, 80, 134,
149, 150, 152
medical physiology and disease
processes, 34
Medical Research Council
(MRC), 33–34, 60–61, 184
medieval and modern history,
31
meeting a supervisor, 45, 46, 58,
70, 71, 73–74, 89
mental health disorders, 34
methodology, 22–23, 89
metrics, *see* Research Assessment
Exercise
micro- and nano engineering,
32
microelectronics, *see* electronics
Migraine Trust, 41, 143, 180
modelling and simulation, 35,
40, 80, 148
modern languages and
linguistics, see languages
money, see debt, fees, funding
MSc (Master of Science)
before PhD, 5, 6, 7, 8, 37, 45,
66, 68, 75, 81, 82, 97,
102, 107
transfer 6, 8
museum studies, *see* librarianship, information and
museum studies
music and performing arts, *see*
arts
nanotechnology and nano
engineering, *see* micro- and
nano engineering
National Graduate Committee,
185
National Endowment for
Science, Technology and
the Arts (NESTA), 184
National Institute for Environmental e-Science, 35

Natural Environment Research
Council (NERC), 34–35,
134, 184
National Lottery Charities
Council, 184
neurological disorders, 34
neuroscience and mental health,
33, 34
New Route PhDs, 7, 11, 46, 145,
149–152
New Route PhD Participating
Universities, 149–152
nondestructive evaluation, 147
nutrition, 34
offer
conditional, 47, 48, 102, 154
unconditional 102, 103, 104,
105, 154
offer letter, 103
Office of Science and Technology, 30, 33, 137, 160
oral health (dentistry), 14, 34,
149, 151, 152
originality, original contribution, 6, 12, 13, 15–16, 21,
69, 73, 83
other diseases and basic
research, 34
Overseas Research Students
Awards Scheme (ORSAS),
37–38, 48, 49, 154–159
part-time, *see* studying
personality of supervisors, 71–73
personality traits, 5–6, 71–72
Particle Physics and Astronomy
Research Council (PPARC),
35, 60, 61, 184
Pathological Society, 143
people and population studies,
33
PhD
aims, 15
in arts and humanities, *see*
arts and humanities
game, 10
interview, *see* interview
New Route, *see* New Route
PhDs
offer, *see* offer letter
requirements, *see* eligibility
in the sciences, *see* sciences
split, *see* New Route PhDs

PhD – *contd*
  thesis, *see* thesis
  types of, *see* doctorate
  what do you do, 24–26
philosophy, law and religious
    studies, 31
photonics, 147
physical sciences, 149, 150, 151,
    152
  see also EPSRC
physics, 33
  see also PPARC
politics, 28–30
plant and microbial sciences, 31
Plymouth Marine Laboratory, 35
post-1992 universities, 54, 58
presentations, *see* public
    speaking
Proudman Oceanographic
    Laboratory, 34
principle investigators, 78, 79
proposal, *see* research proposal
public engagement, 33, 184
public speaking, 100, 126,
    127–128
qualifications, *see* eligibility
radar, 32
radio communications, 32
reasons, 2–5, 109, 119
records, *see* documentation
red-brick universities, 51–52
research agency webpages, 184
Research Assessment Exercise
    (RAE), 62, 63, 64
research councils
  AHRC, *see* Arts and
      Humantities Research
      Council
  BBSRC, *see* Biotechnology
      and Biological Sciences
      Research Council
  CCLRC, *see* Council for the
      Central Laboratory of
      the Research Councils
  ESRC, *see* Economic and
      Social Research Council
  EPSRC, *see* Engineering and
      Physical Sciences
      Research Council
  MRC, *see* Medical Research
      Council

research councils – *contd*
  NERC, *see* Natural Environ-
      ment Research Council
  PPARC, *see* Particle Physics
      and Astronomy Research
      Council
The Research Council (RCUK),
    184
research project, 3, 5, 21, 30, 37,
    43, 45, 70, 81–90, 96, 104,
    119
research proposal
  for funding application, 36,
      37, 39, 155, 157
  for PhD application, 44, 45,
      69, 81, 83–90, 155, 157
reproductive health, 34
Royal Academy of Engineering
    (RAEng), 137
Royal Society, 137, 138
Royal Society of Chemistry, 134
Royal Society of Edinburgh,
    143–144
scholarships
  British Council, 48–49, 133
  British Marshall, *see* British
      Marshall Scholarships
  commonwealth, *see* Common-
      wealth Scholarship
      Commission
  Fulbright, *see* Fulbright
      Scholarships
  non-UK, 153–165
  School of Oriental and African
      Studies Scholarships, 137,
      164
SCIART, 184
sciences, 1, 6, 8, 12, 13, 14, 16,
    17, 19, 21, 22, 25, 28, 31,
    32, 33, 34, 37, 39, 57, 58,
    61, 63, 67, 83, 98, 100, 133,
    134, 135, 137, 140, 141,
    142, 147, 148, 149, 150,
    151, 152, 184
Scottish Association for Marine
    Science, 35
Sea Mammal Research Unit, 35
second supervisors, 80
short visits, *see* small awards
small awards, 136–138
social stability and exclusion, 33

space facilities, *see* ground and space-based facilities
specialist studentship webpages, 134–135
stress, 8, 9, 25–26, 28, 55, 57, 124–125
student
  mature, 9, 84, 111
  halls, *see* university accommodation
housing, *see* accommodation
visas, *see* visa
studentships
  advertised, 37, 43, 44–48, 57, 132–135
  CASE, 42–43, 46–47, 145
  charity, 47, 139–144
  international, *see* funding international, scholarships
  quota, 36, 45, 47, 48, 155
studying
  different ways of, 23–24
  full-time, 11, 23, 43, 53, 103, 105, 106, 154, 155, 167
  part-time 11, 23–24, 53, 103, 107
supervisor
  career, 36, 77–79
  changing, *see* changing your supervisor
  contacting, *see* contacting a supervisor
  experience, *see* experience of a supervisor
  finding, *see* finding a supervisor
  meeting, *see* meeting a supervisor
  personality, *see* personality of supervisors
  second, *see* second supervisors
  time, 58, 73–74
Synchrotron Radiation Source, 32
systematic enquiry, 16–17
talks, *see* public speaking
technology development, 32
telecommunications, *see* communications technology
tenancy agreement, 113–115
theoretical biology, 32

thesis, 1, 11, 13, 15, 16, 18, 19, 20, 21, 22, 26, 57, 68, 73, 83, 102, 108, 109, 117, 118, 119, 120, 121, 122, 123–124, 125, 128
Tibawi Trust, 137
transfer masters, *see* MSc
transfer viva, 73, 118
transport, 148
UK, *see* fees, funding, scholarships, studentships
UK GRAD programme, 186
university
  accommodation, *see* accommodation
  ancient, *see* ancient universities
  campus-based, *see* campus-based universities
  city, *see* city-based universities
  cultures, 25, 58–60
  directory, 176–177
  facilities, 23, 24, 27, 29, 32, 35, 54, 55, 56, 58, 65
  glass-plate, *see* glass-plate universities
  judging, 60–65
  lists, *see* tables
  location, 55–57
  modern, *see* post-1992 universities
  new, *see* post-1992 and glass-plate universities
  old, *see* ancient universities
  post-1992, *see* post-1992 universities
  research performance indicators, *see* HEFCE research performance indicators
RAE, *see* Research Assessment Exercise
red-brick, *see* red-brick universities
tables, 51, 52, 53, 54, 61, 62, 63, 64
webpages, *see* directory
visa, 3, 24, 96, 104–106, 108, 166–174
vision and hearing, 34
visual arts and media, *see* arts

viva voca, 16, 17, 18, 73, 89, 102, 118, 119, 128

water science, 147, 150

webpages
    of charities, *see* charity webpages
    for information and advice, *see* information and advice webpages

webpages – *contd*
    of research agencies, *see* research agency webpages
    of universities, *see* university webpages
    see also internet
Wellcome Trust, 40, 42, 140, 164, 165, 183
work and organisation, 33
writing, 67, 68, 69, 83–90, 100, 117, 120, 121, 126–127